A GIFT FOR ADMIRATION

Further Memoirs

JAMES LORD

A GIFT FOR ADMIRATION

Further Memoirs

Farrar • Straus • Giroux / New York

Farrar, Straus and Giroux
19 Union Square West, New York 10003

Library of Congress Cataloging-in-Publication Data
Lord, James.
    A gift for admiration : further memoirs / James Lord. — 1st ed.
    p. cm.
    ISBN 0-374-28192-0 (alk. paper)
    1. Art patrons—Biography.   2. Artists—Biography.   I. Title.
NX701.L67   1998
700'.92'2—dc21
[B]   97-50205

FOR GILLES

CONTENTS

1. One Joyful Millionaire ❧ Henry McIlhenny

3

2. Sudbury Cottage ❧ Isabel Rawsthorne

43

3. A Palace in the City of Love and Death ❧ Peggy Guggenheim

85

4. Beyond Horizon ❧ Sonia Orwell and Peter Watson

113

5. A Firefly in the Meadow ❧ Ethel Bliss Platt

143

Envoi

177

Index

191

Part One

ONE JOYFUL MILLIONAIRE

HENRY MCILHENNY

Going from Glenveagh to the movies was no expedition to be undertaken on the spur of the moment. To begin with, the distance from the castle to the gate was five miles, and at the gate you were next to nowhere, the nearest village being Churchill, several miles farther on. The cinema was located in a town considerably more distant, en route to which one had to pass through an insignificant little place called Milford. As we drove through it one evening in 1963, Henry pointed out a poor cottage on the left-hand side of the road and said, "That's where my grandfather was born. Thank God he left when he was fourteen. Before the famine. If he'd stayed on and died . . . well, my dear, no gas meter, no Henry, and no Glenveagh. What a loss to civilization!" He chuckled vivaciously, a laugh rising from deep in his throat, which exemplified one of the most appealing traits of his character: a candor about himself so unassuming that it became easy for him to take lightly what he also took with enthusiastic seriousness.

Glenveagh Castle stands in County Donegal at the edge of a large, lonely, romantic lake in the far northwestern corner of the Republic of Ireland not far from the sea. Huge and ugly, it was built of local granite in the midst of the Victorian era by a man called Adair, known locally as Black Adair by evicted tenant farmers, who hated and eventually murdered him because of his callous clearing of 32,000 acres to create a deer park and pleasure grounds adjoining the castle. After his murder the place was neglected for decades, but it had been built by a man avid for permanence and withstood neglect in tolerably good repair. Late in the 1920s it was bought by a professor of art history at Harvard, where Henry was then a student, named Kingsley Porter. His fate might have led a superstitious person to fancy that Black Adair had cast an evil spell upon the premises. One summer's day in 1933 Porter, his wife, and some friends went for a picnic to a small island near the coast. Having finished his meal, the professor set off by himself for a stroll. He was never seen again. When he did not return, his wife and friends searched the island back and forth in vain till nightfall. Not a trace of the man or his clothing was to be found, and the boat which had brought them to the island that morning remained undisturbed where it had been moored. Porter's disappearance seemed inexplicable. He had been in excellent health and good spirits, while his private and professional life gave no cause for worry. His body was never found. Under such circumstances, it is not surprising that Mrs. Porter felt no desire to reside any longer at Glenveagh.

Frances McIlhenny, Henry's mother, was not a superstitious person. An energetic widow of great wealth, aged sixty-four, she knew what she wanted and was accustomed to getting it. Learning from her son of Porter's disappearance, she determined to rent his castle for the following summer. Her father-in-law, as she was well aware, had been born nearby and it was he who had founded the great family fortune by inventing—and patenting!—the gas meter at a time when most of the homes in American cities were lighted by gas and kitchen stoves fueled by it. Perhaps some atavistic sense of a return to familial origins prompted her impulse. At all events, both she and her son, indifferent to the fates of previous inhabitants, fell in love with Glenveagh, the bleak splendor and almost Wagnerian magic of the site. Three years later, aged only twenty-seven, Henry bought the castle and all its 32,000 acres for just $25,000. He owned the estate for forty-six years and, except for the interruption of World War II, spent several months there every summer, deriving great pleasure from the place and providing great pleasure to innumerable guests, of whom I was lucky enough on several occasions to be one.

It was Harold Acton who first introduced me to Henry McIlhenny in Florence in May 1951. From Harold, who relished relating the minutiae, scandalous if possible, of other people's lives, I learned the background of Henry's. He had been born about 1910 in Philadelphia, where his family, thanks to their wealth, rubbed shoulders with the time-honored elite of a city which had been the first capital of the young republic, and calculated the honor of time with exacting discrimination. Admittedly, the McIlhennys were nouveaux riches, but their richesse was so considerable, their manners so impeccable, and their mansion in outlying Germantown so vast that polite allowances were made. The senior McIlhenny bought up public utilities, caught the collecting fever, acquiring many second-rate Dutch paintings and a large collection of Oriental carpets, some of them considered masterpieces, which he bequeathed to the Philadelphia Museum of Art, of which he became president during the last few years of his life. His children had also caught the collecting fever by the time their father died. While still at Harvard, Henry, subsidized by a doting mother, was able to decorate his rooms with an important painting by Chardin and drawings by Seurat and Matisse, a promising start for a collection which eventually became one of the most distinguished, if not the largest, in America. Throughout the thirties, always aided by his mother, who did not die until 1943, Henry added great pictures by David, Ingres, Cézanne, Renoir, Degas,

Toulouse-Lautrec, Vuillard, Rouault, and Picasso. He even owned an unexpectedly good little painting by Dalí.

His presence in Florence in the spring of 1951 was due to his acquisition of a fine townhouse in the fashionable center of Philadelphia at 1914 Rittenhouse Square. Life in the suburbs was not for Henry, and the mansion of his parents had been half emptied by bequests to the museum and sales necessary for settlement of the estate. While the house on Rittenhouse Square was being renovated, Henry had come to Florence to attend the May music festival before going on to Glenveagh. He and his friend Angus Menzies shared a villa rented from an English noblewoman named Lady Lauder, where I was several times invited with Harold to jolly dinners attended by men only. And that is how Henry and I became friendly. I was attracted and entertained by his good nature, urbane but unpretentious sophistication, sincere concern for art, and highly entertaining gossip about the grand, rich, and famous, whose acquaintance he cultivated. There is no question about it: Henry was great fun. And yet there was something elusive about him, too, a reserve which suggested that he would—or, perhaps, could—never completely surrender to another person the entire dimension of his innermost being. His self-possession was such, however, that one could hardly doubt that he took the measure of this dimension quite realistically and did not trouble himself about its limitations or flatter himself over its extent. In short, there was something of a mystery about Henry. It roused one's curiosity and may have made him more interesting than he superficially seemed. The interest, one felt, lay concealed somewhere between the apparent persona of the flighty and amusing international playboy and the highly knowledgeable, refined connoisseur of art. I don't believe that many of Henry's friends, who were virtually countless, gave much thought to this curious dichotomy, being too dazzled by his glamour or appreciative of his good taste. But it struck me almost from the beginning as the key—if one could only find it and place it in the proper lock—which would open the door to the hiding place of Henry's secret self. I'm not a bit sure I can come close to doing this, but it may prove illuminating to try.

Probably it was a bit of luck for the young Henry that his father died when he was only fifteen, as McIlhenny *père* seems to have been a rather stiff, reserved, and stern individual, forty-four years old when his youngest child was born, preoccupied by business, less refined and educated than his wife. Although he acquired a taste for collecting—mainly for the sake of social éclat—he cared more for finance, golf, and fishing, and one may guess that he would not have been disposed to spend enormous sums for the masterpieces coveted by his son or to encourage him to lead what looked like a life of unproductive leisure. The mother was both indulgent and prescient. Even at age ten, Henry impressed her with his enthusiasm for works of art, his precocious knowledge of art history, and his discerning taste, which was very akin to her own, especially concerning silver and furniture. As for the appreciation of great French art, it was the son who educated the mother, going about it at times with some asperity. Between the two, however, no serious dispute ever arose, though upon occasion maternal serenity entailed filial disappointment. Henry's older siblings, Bernice, always known as Bonnie, and John, who died young, were never keen or conscientious about collecting. Bonnie in time, aided by gifts from her brother, one of them a superb painting by Matisse, gathered a considerable collection of silver and pictures, many of these second-rate Picassos, but she sold nearly everything at auction well before her death. Like her father, she was rather stern and an addicted golfer. She married a weak and depressive man named Wintersteen, bore four sons, and dourly endured her husband's suicidal monitions until he did finally do away with himself. Henry lived in the great world of high culture and high society, while Bonnie played bridge and golf. As brother and sister they were fond of each other, but a disinterested observer might well have thought that they were united more by memories and money than by deep familial devotion. I saw Bonnie seldom, and it seemed clear to me that she tolerated Henry's friends with reluctant politeness rather than good-tempered interest. To be sure, Henry must have been an embarrassment to her. Never did it occur to him to live in any other city than the one in which he had been born and brought up. Nor did it ever occur to him that he need be assiduously secretive about the reason which made it unthinkable that he should marry. He did not throw this in the face of Philadelphia society, never lived openly with another man, but he discreetly declined to hide that important truth about himself. If people knew—and everybody did—they were welcome to take it amiss, but when he gave parties for Princess Margaret, Brooke Astor, or Tennessee Williams, they set aside prejudice and hurried to attend if invited.

It was while still in his early twenties at Harvard that Henry decided what purpose in life he would pursue, and he pursued it with astute perseverance for half a century. He would make himself a connoisseur and collector of nineteenth-century and early-twentieth-century French art, encouraged in this resolve by the legendary professor of fine arts at Harvard, Paul J. Sachs. His choice was dictated both by personal taste and by practical acumen. He knew that the McIlhenny fortune, though considerable, could not compete with those of Andrew Mellon, J. P. Morgan, Jules Bache, and like clients of the redoubtable Joe Duveen. Thus, the acquisition of Old Masters was excluded. But that didn't trouble Henry, because he had cleverly realized that a great collection was not made by great names but by great pictures and that these need not be many if they were of the very highest quality. Besides, he did not hanker to live with Dürers, Titians, Rembrandts, Pieros, or El Grecos. The situation regarding relatively recent French pictures was quite different, especially during the Depression years, when many collectors

were compelled to part with masterpieces in order to make both
ends continue to meet in comfort. By limiting himself almost
entirely to works of the previous century, Henry made his task
both simpler and more difficult. Many paintings were still to be
had at prices he could afford or, to be more specific, at prices
his mother was willing to pay, encouraged, and sometimes
goaded, by her excitable son. The difficulty lay in determining
precisely which pictures were the very finest among the many
available. Henry made very few mistakes. One of them was one
of his very first purchases, a Delacroix portrait of a handsome
youth, a weak picture altogether uncharacteristic of Delacroix's
mature style, but Henry may be forgiven for having erred when
only twenty-two for the sake of a good-looking boy. He quickly
made up for this minor error by persuading his mother
within a year to acquire masterpieces by Renoir, Delacroix,
and Cézanne. And the two together had already before this
bought Toulouse-Lautrec's greatest painting, *The Dance at the
Moulin-Rouge*. The enlightened connoisseur, however, must
know how to wait, and it was not until well after Mrs. Mc-
Ilhenny's death in 1943 that the collection attained its ultimate
greatness.

Frances McIlhenny was a lady of considerable reserve, but she
was a woman wise in the ways of society. In her circles, unmar-
ried young men were fairly numerous, but indiscreet questions
as to their private inclinations were never asked. To be a bachelor, especially a rich one, may have been deemed uncustomary,
especially by mothers with eligible daughters, but no stigma attached to a young man so long as he kept out of trouble. What
Mrs. McIlhenny knew or guessed about her son's propensities
we will never learn, but it may be apt to recall that she was
already twenty-six years old at the time of the Oscar Wilde scandal. Very little in public attitudes toward homosexuality had
changed by the time she died. Her son, at least, lived to see and
to enjoy a radical shift toward increased tolerance. But his

mother cannot have known that that would ever occur. When she came to draw her will, she may have had this in mind. Her son, only thirty-three when she died, was bequeathed a very considerable fortune, but the great majority of the capital was left untouchable in strictly entailed trusts, which would pass without reservation to Bonnie's four sons when Henry, if childless, came to die. The pictures, of course, the real estate, silver, and furniture all went to him outright, and when he did die forty-three years later, the value of all this was virtually incalculable. If Mrs. McIlhenny feared that her son might have frivolously squandered the capital or spent it on undeserving, and unpresentable, companions, she very much misjudged his character. True, Henry spent freely for his own enjoyment, which usually gave enjoyment to his friends, for as a host he was as refined and conscientious as he was when judging the aesthetic merits of a work of art. Still, the rigid stipulations of the mother's will ultimately led to the loss of two masterpieces which she would have been sad to see disappear from her son's residence.

Soon after leaving Harvard, where he had flourished under the intimidating wing of Professor Sachs, Henry joined the curatorial staff of the Philadelphia Museum of Art in the department of decorative arts. This suited him perfectly, because his forte was good taste as the measure of an ideally harmonious ensemble. Though he had relatively little to do with the department of paintings, he kept an eye on acquisitions, loaned works from his own collection when needed, and sometimes lent a helping hand to the arrangement of important exhibitions. During the war he spent four years of rather monotonous service in the navy, rising to the rank of lieutenant commander. Discharged in 1946, he returned at once to Philadelphia and to his duties at the museum. His last great acquisition, this one without maternal aid or advice, came three years later: van Gogh's *Rain*. A masterful view from the window of the painter's room in the asylum at St.-Rémy, it depicts the walled field outside and the mountains beyond drenched by wintry, blue streaks of rain, a haunting image of melancholy genius.

My first visit to 1914 Rittenhouse Square took place on the 29th of April, 1952, less than a year after I'd made Henry's acquaintance in Florence. Little could I have imagined then, aged twenty-nine, that during the thirty-four years to come before Henry's death, despite my numerous, lengthy sojourns in Europe, I would again be a guest in that prodigious house on twenty-two occasions. That first time I was on my way to Washington and had telephoned Henry, hoping that he would invite me for a drink so that I could see his collection, and instead he asked me to come to dinner and stay overnight. 1914 was not nearly so splendid at the time as it later became and could hardly compare with palatial mansions like that of Marie-Laure de Noailles. Standing at a corner of the square, it was, and still is, a four-story brick structure of no particular distinction, neither ugly nor beautiful. To the rear lay a small garden, overlooked by a homely little two-story house immediately next door. Though not so grand as it was to become, Henry's home in those first years was decidedly more formal than in its final phase. Two imposing figures presided over it with almost more autonomy, it seemed, than the proprietor. The first was the butler, a tall, portly personage well past middle age, white-haired but spry, named Henry Fussey. His surname suited him. During the day he was attired in a swallow-tailed morning coat, striped trousers, and pearl-gray necktie. At dinner, assisted by a footman in a plain black suit, Mr. Fussey was resplendent in full evening dress. Given a few medals and a blue ribbon across his immaculate shirtfront, he would have added distinction to a ball at Buckingham Palace. His employer was quite proud of him, relating with some solemnity that he had formerly served the gran-

diose Stotesburys in their suburban palace at Chestnut Hill. The
other essential person in the household at 1914 was Henry's
secretary, a middle-aged lady of terse and impeccable efficiency
named Mrs. Heritage, whose maiden name had been Rich, a
fact highly entertaining to Henry. He always had breakfast in
bed, where his mail was brought to him, and when he had per-
used it, Heritage would be summoned to take down in short-
hand all replies that politesse did not require to be handwritten.
She also sent out the invitations to Henry's many parties, arranged with caterers, paid bills and servants, and rivaled Mr.
Fussey as indispensable superintendent of the household.
Though I don't think I ever saw either one of them smile, I
suppose it must have seemed to Henry that he couldn't get
along without their services. Eventually he had to, and it seemed
to some of his friends that he didn't get along quite as well as
he should have.

Henry took his work as curator at the museum with committed seriousness, although he allowed himself five or six months
of vacation every year. Even while abroad, however, he kept a
falcon's eye on the lookout for suitable additions to the museum's collection, many of which he paid for himself. He even
prevailed upon a collector as cautiously possessive as Charles de
Noailles to donate to the museum a series of splendid Brussels
tapestries. After the war, he organized several landmark exhibitions of Philadelphia furniture, silver, and porcelain in collabo-
ration with his assistant and crony, a young fellow named Louis
Madeira, who had married the only child of a man whose home
contained half a dozen Cézannes, Renoir's magnificent *Grandes
Baigneuses*, several Manets, and van Gogh's greatest version of
The Sunflowers. The curator of paintings at the museum was also
one of Henry's dependable pals. Indeed, Philadelphia boasted,
or gingerly made the best, of quite a few jolly gentlemen of
fashion. Older and more tolerant than New York, less inhibited
than Boston, it could afford to do so with good grace as long

as nothing on the surface appeared too conspicuously out of order. And as the decades passed, the degree of conspicuousness that could be accepted with good grace became more and more explicit.

After Henry Fussey's retirement, things were never again the same at 1914 Rittenhouse Square. For one thing, the mansion became grander. Henry was able to acquire the small two-story house overlooking the garden. In order to do so, he was obliged to sell a picture, and he chose to get rid of the worst one he had: a very late Renoir, *The Judgment of Paris*, its roseate, over-inflated ladies weightily posing in a slipshod landscape. He had the next-door building demolished, using the extra space to create a handsome, domed entrance hall and doubling the size of his principal drawing room, which provided a more satisfactory viewing perspective for the largest painting in his collection, a life-size double portrait by David of Pope Pius VII and Cardinal Caprara, studies for the immense but inaccurate portrayal of Napoleon's coronation. The elimination of neighbors also encouraged him to improve his garden, adding large rhododendron and camellia bushes, plus a fountain with a white marble sculpture of the birth of Venus and two dolphins spitting streams of water into a pool.

And then there was a new butler. During his summer excursions abroad Henry inevitably became acquainted with the so-called international set, men and women of wealth and outstanding social éclat either inherited or purchased. In July of 1953, for example, I found myself staying at the estate of Lady Kenmare and her son Rory Cameron at St.-Jean-Cap-Ferrat, a Palladian villa called La Fiorentina set on a peninsula overlooking the Mediterranean. I was the guest of Rory, of course, as were Henry and Angus Menzies. But Lady Kenmare was more interesting, a great beauty even at an advanced age, Australian by birth, who boasted of having possessed not a single pair of shoes before the age of sixteen yet who was married four times to increasingly rich husbands, all of whom thoughtfully expired shortly after wedlock, leaving the widow wealthier and wealthier. Somerset Maugham, a near neighbor, said that he'd like to write a book about her but desisted because her presence at the bridge table meant more to him than one more novel. Henry visited places like St.-Tropez, Salzburg, Paris, London, Rio, India, Honolulu, Hong Kong, and Palm Beach, naturally meeting everybody everywhere who was anybody anywhere, plus quite a few nobodies to enliven his sojourns. In addition he invited to Glenveagh, even to Rittenhouse Square, multitudes of people encountered here and there across the world. So it was not surprising that a new butler was recruited as a consequence of fashionable international jaunts. Before coming to 1914, this man had been butler aboard one of the most luxurious yachts afloat upon the Mediterranean, the *Gaviota*, property of a South American millionaire named Arturo López, a small, ugly man famous for maintaining his boyfriends in sumptuous style, though he had married, in an ostentatious and cynical effort to keep up appearances. The new butler represented a serious, indeed astonishing, descent in standards from the style of Mr. Fussey. I can't remember his name, but I can't forget his manner. He was familiar and none too fastidious in demeanor. Habits formed on López's yacht cannot have been easy to break. Gone were the days of swallowtail coats. Gone, too, not long after his arrival, was Mrs. Heritage. The new secretary turned out to be a pleasant, easygoing, colorless young woman. It was now Henry who entirely controlled the management of his household. If things were less formal, if the butler laughed out loud at jokes told by guests while he was serving dinner, the host did not seem to mind.

Henry was seriously concerned not only with art but also with every cultural aspect of his era. For many years he was on the boards of the Philadelphia Orchestra, one of the country's finest, and of the Metropolitan Opera. He went frequently to New

York to the theater, rarely missing a production of merit. His contributions to charity were considerable and regular in support of medical and scientific research, educational institutions, the preservation of various species of wild animals threatened with extinction, and other meritorious causes. Both of his residences were well stocked with books of all sorts. He made lists of recent publications to be purchased, often in duplicate, one copy for each house, and he read almost all of them. Trash was not tolerated even at Glenveagh, where a few thrillers might have helped to pass away long afternoons that were almost always rainy. Henry's corner of Donegal was the rainiest region in all of Ireland, which could be tedious for guests but was wonderful for the glorious gardens.

I don't think Henry was ever lonely, though as a solitary bachelor he was often alone. Certainly he never gave the slightest impression of being morose. It has been said that happiness is elusive for the possessors of great fortunes, especially for those who have inherited them. Not for Henry. He had hundreds of friends scattered across the world and these included not only princes and dukes but also numerous poets, musicians, actors, and dancers, even movie stars. They enjoyed his company and he very openly enjoyed theirs. An exceptionally genial host, he was one of the most entertaining men one could hope to know, with an extraordinary store of amusing anecdotes, witty gossip, and Jamesian tales about his world, which, indeed, was a lineal descendant of the Master's. He liked people for themselves, and if his guests were sometimes boring, as they could be, he knew how to liven them up. And yet it never seemed to me that he was truly intimate with anyone. It happened occasionally both in Ireland and in Philadelphia that I spent a few days alone with him. He knew how to keep calmly to himself, read, see to the proper maintenance of his estate, take long hikes across the bogs, or listen to records of music for the solo violin given him by his friend Yehudi Menuhin. Conversations *à deux* were lively at luncheon and dinner. We talked about art and art dealers, the prices of works of art, about mutual friends and about their friends, scandals old and new, politics and humdrum topics of the moment. One topic, I noticed, we never talked about: love. Oh, we discussed the affairs of our friends, of course, but never our own. I would have been perfectly willing, but my willingness would have seemed to take for granted a response in kind from Henry, and I sensed that he was unprepared to be frank about such matters. It seemed impossible to imagine that Henry had ever said to any human being, "I love you." When we first met, he was with Angus, and it seemed evident that they had been lovers. But Angus, living in London, saw Henry only intermittently. I think there had previously been someone else in Henry's life, but I never knew much about that. In thirty-five years of acquaintance and many meetings, the only affair I had an opportunity to observe in person was the one with Aleco. His is a strange, improbable story, with sensational twists and turns, worth relating for its own extravagant anecdotal interest.

Every summer Henry took a vacation from the romantic, rainy isolation of Glenveagh. Sometimes he went to Salzburg for the music festival, sometimes to Venice, and sometimes to Montecatini for the cure, which did him no good whatsoever, since he was an unrepentant and insatiable gourmet. And sometimes he indulged himself and guests in a pleasure reserved for those who never have to count the cost: he hired a luxurious yacht and cruised among the Greek islands. This was the diversion he chose about 1960. Of his ports of call that summer, one of the first was the small island of Hydra, a picturesque spot much beloved by the lotus-eating class, some of whom maintained luxurious homes along the steep, narrow streets. Henry's yacht was too large to be moored against the jetty, and dropped anchor late one afternoon well out in the harbor. Inevitably, it attracted attention. Now, as it happened, there was located in Hydra at that time an academy that trained select young men to become officers in the Greek merchant marine. Eyeing the sleek craft which had just arrived in their harbor, several of these young fellows, wanting a closer look, and perhaps motivated by more obscure expectations, decided to swim out to it. Their splashings and chatterings naturally attracted the attention of those on board, whereupon Henry instructed his captain to invite the swimmers to climb the ship's ladder and join his guests on deck for a drink. The agile cadets were aboard in a minute, dripping wet in their brief bathing suits. Henry ordered up terry-cloth bathrobes for all and they sat down astern, where drinks were served. The occasion was amusing and unexpected, but its jollity was somewhat diminished by the fact that only one of the cadets spoke passable English. By a happy chance, however, the linguist was far and away the best-looking boy of the lot, with curly dark hair, lean, tanned features, sparkling teeth, black eyes, and beneath the terry-cloth robe a slender but muscular physique in the tradition of Praxiteles. His real name was not Aleco, but we will call him that. His chance swim that summer afternoon changed his life forever and led to a series of phenomenal adventures which nothing in the world could have prepared him to anticipate.

He must at the time have been about eighteen. His affable manner, ready talk, and easy smile, however, made him seem more mature. He came from a modest bourgeois background, had received an acceptable education, but did not look forward with equanimity to marrying a presentable girl of his class and settling down to an uneventful family life in Athens. He wanted to travel abroad, visit exotic lands, and prepare himself, if possible, for a life more exciting and interesting than would probably have fallen to his lot at home. That is why he had thought to join the merchant marine and applied himself to the study of conversational English. It may not therefore have been altogether a thoughtless whim that had led him to swim out for a closer look at Henry's yacht. And it was natural enough, once on board, that he should conduct himself so as not to appear in the least intimidated by a first encounter with luxury of international style. This slight hint of sophistication was not lost, of course, on Henry, nor was he indifferent to the outstanding good looks of his guest. When it came time for the other cadets to swim back to shore, Aleco was invited to stay aboard for dinner. He accepted and a suitable outfit was gotten together. After dinner, drinks, and talk, the other guests having retired to their cabins, Henry suggested that if it would not interfere with his course of training, Aleco might care to remain overnight. The suggestion meant what it was intended to mean, for this was still the era when Greek girls were strictly chaperoned and young men accepted more or less as a matter of course a period of compliant homosexuality. And then, of course, there was the powerful lure of the yacht. Aleco said he'd be happy to stay overnight, and there is no reason to suppose his happiness was feigned. I think he was far too vain to be bothered about the pretense.

The next morning Henry looked upon his handsome good luck and wondered whether it might not be made to last a bit longer. It might be a gamble, yes, but he could withdraw his investment fairly quickly if necessary and it was not, in any case, very high. Besides, he was by nature impulsively generous and imagined that some lasting good might come to Aleco from more intimate acquaintance. Accordingly, he proposed that if his fortuitous guest could obtain leave from the merchant marine academy, perhaps he would enjoy staying aboard the yacht for the remainder of the cruise, which was to last for a couple of weeks longer, visiting several islands and running up the Turkish coast. Aleco, one might say, flung himself at the opportunity. Leave would be easy to obtain, because the men in training were under no obligation to complete the course should they find that they possessed no seagoing vocation. So the young fellow went ashore in the yacht's speedboat, presented himself to his commandant, was granted temporary leave, gathered his gear, and returned aboard in time for lunch. The yacht presently weighed anchor, having been in Hydra harbor less than twenty-four hours, and Aleco never again saw the merchant marine academy.

The cruise was a great success. If anyone, either lady or gentleman, glanced askance at the new member of the party, it was with surpassing discretion. Henry was delighted. Aleco proved in every sense to be a pleasurable and entertaining companion. He had an instinctive sense of how to make himself agreeable. Having brought along a guitar, he could sing a few traditional Greek songs and execute the intricate solo dances popular among his countrymen. His youthful exuberance much enlivened the cruise for everyone aboard. When it was over, Henry suggested that Aleco might like to accompany him for the rest of the summer to Glenveagh. The answer, of course, was yes. After the yacht the castle, where Henry employed fifty servants indoors and out, must have appeared to the youth from a colorless background in Athens like an ancient myth come to life, with himself as Ganymede and Henry the omnipotent eagle. And no aspect of the situation apparently seemed, either to the shepherd or to the god, at all displeasing or unseemly. And so, the summer having sped by, Henry proposed that Aleco accompany him to America, the country of all countries where Greeks long, and expect, to gather golden apples. It was specified from the beginning, however, that Aleco would not be expected to live in Philadelphia. Henry would never have accepted an arrangement which publicly proclaimed that he had provided himself with a kept boy. Aleco would be installed in an apartment in New York, and visit Philadelphia on weekends. This arrangement suited both parties very nicely. Henry could continue as an upright pillar, so to speak, of Philadelphia society, while Aleco explored the opportunities of Manhattan, and from Friday evening till Sunday afternoon the two could enjoy each other in the company of understanding guests like myself and many another sympathetic soul. Something constructive, of course, had to be found for Aleco to do. Henry believed, and expected, from the first that Aleco should make the most of this prodigious chance to forge a constructive and independent existence for himself. He liked to sing and dance, had had adolescent dreams of appearing on the stage, so Henry arranged for him to be enrolled in a school for aspiring actors. His apartment on the Upper East Side was comfortable without being luxurious—its only work of art a photo of a Cézanne drawing that hung in Henry's bedroom—but he gave convivial parties there for selected schoolmates, the majority of whom very soon proved to be girls.

And so things went for a few years. Aleco was seen during the summers here and there with Henry but never as a permanent or inevitable companion. His theatrical studies led to no appearances on Broadway, or Off-Broadway, stages, but frequently provided lengthy performances of popular songs on Saturday nights at 1914. A tiny fly in this hedonistic ointment occasionally called attention to itself in the form of official notices from Athens to the effect that the young Aleco had not presented himself for the term of military training compulsory in Greece. If he had completed the course at the merchant marine academy, he would have been excused from this requirement, but that opportunity had slipped by. Henry, needless to say, knew people in Washington, and deferment was easily obtained. Nobody worried, least of all Aleco. During the week in New York he was having a very good time. He had met a lot of people, especially the trashy bohemian Andy Warhol crowd that hung out at Max's Kansas City; he gave good parties in his cozy apartment and had an affair with an exotic sculptress. Sometimes now there were weekends when he did not turn up in Philadelphia, and sometimes when he did turn up, he drank too much and grew a little surly. I remember one evening when Henry gently suggested

the uselessness of yet another drink, whereupon Aleco gruffly
exclaimed that he was not in the habit of taking orders,
wrenched from his wrist a very fine watch, a gift from his host,
and flung it across the room. Luckily, it hit the drawn draperies,
not the wall, and slid undamaged to the floor. Henry remained
imperturbable. If there were remonstrances, they were made in
private. But it did seem to us all that the original gleam of the
relationship showed signs of tarnish. And this was confirmed by
Henry himself, who made no secret of the fact that Aleco had
informed him without qualification that their physical relations
were at an end.

Henry accepted all this with outward serenity. He was a
superlatively practical and sensible man, his good judgment
adapted to the great world in which he spent most of his life as
well as to the fractional slice of the demimonde to which he had
been drawn by nature. If Aleco was brought to America in the
first instance to satisfy Henry's pleasure, there had certainly been
on the part of his benefactor an expectation that a large amount
of leisure, as he knew from his own experience, could be put to
fructifying purpose. When he found that this was not to be, he
must have been disappointed. What had happened was simply
that the youth had become a man. Nothing, of course, in his
background or experience could have prepared him to make a
purposeful and fruitful life from the opportunity which chance
had pressed upon him. Nobody is to blame for being ordinary,
yet it requires a deft touch of instinct to manage the corkscrew
of fate so that it opens prodigious vintages. Unbeknownst to
himself, Aleco possessed a touch, but first a period of pathless
probation would test his fortitude.

Still another peremptory message arrived from Athens order-
ing Aleco to report for military training. This time Henry said
that he might as well go and get it over with rather than let
Damocles' sword dangle indefinitely. To Aleco it may have
seemed that he was being callously cast off for discreditable rea-

sons. If so, he had not taken the true measure of Henry's character, as he would learn later, to his enduring benefit. The
homecoming, however, was morose. He managed to obtain an
easy assignment in Athens but had to live at home, which was
a constraint after whooping it up with Andy and the Walking
Dead at the Factory.

Life in the meantime went on more or less as before at 1914
and Glenveagh Castle. I don't think Aleco was sorely missed,
but he was not forgotten, was spoken of with warmth, and
Henry never failed as a correspondent. A distinct aura of deco-
rum was restored to Henry's residences by the dismissal of Señor
López's onetime butler, who had grown seriously alcoholic and
was occasionally the cause of egregious lapses. His position was
taken by the butler from Glenveagh, a quiet, efficient young man
named Patrick Gallagher, who remained with Henry till the end.
Nobody took Aleco's place, and for the next twenty-odd years,
from the age of fifty-five onward, Henry seemed quite content
to remain without any lasting attachment that could have been
called romantic. In 1964, after thirty years of conscientious service, he retired from his post as curator of decorative arts at the
museum but immediately became a member of the board and
for several years served as its chairman. His collection had by
this time become famous and made him famous, a condition
which he unabashedly enjoyed. "My dear," he used to say, "Ingres and Cézanne are better box office than Rock Hudson and
Lana Turner." He was right. Articles appeared in newspapers
and magazines throughout the Western world. The collection
was exhibited as far afield as San Francisco and throngs of ladies
whose hair, if not stockings, were deep blue applied to visit
1914. Few were turned away. One day Henry was called on the
telephone by a man who had walked by the house and peered
through a drawing-room window. "Isn't that a painting by van
Gogh you've got in your house?" inquired the caller. When told
that it was, he said, "Do you mind if I come by sometime for

a look at the rest of your stuff?" Henry invited the discerning passerby for tea the very next afternoon.

Life at Glenveagh was rather like being aboard an ocean liner in the days of the Windsors, Lady Astor, and Lord Beaverbrook, save that the vessel was made of granite and moored beside a lake as aloof as the ocean itself. Black tie, for example, de rigueur at dinner. There was nothing to do but read, go for hikes in the persistent drizzle, play parlor games, and devour enormous meals of the very finest food I have ever eaten. The food and wine at Glenveagh were, in a word, *incomparable*. And Henry loved to eat. It was Glenveagh that got him grossly overweight at sixty and obese a decade later. And then there were the gardens, which he created out of open fields with the elegant advice of his old friend Lanning Roper. Gardens that led into gardens that led into gardens that led ever farther into ever more luxuriant, exotic, variegated gardens. How many acres there were I suspect even the gardeners couldn't have guessed, as every year for forty-six years, being employed by the year, they added and added till the flower beds and pleasure grounds and hedges and walls and staircases and arches were countless, not to mention the greenhouses and the orangerie, where we often sipped our coffee after lunch. It was a wonderland. When occasionally the sun shone for a few hours, what ineffable delight to wander about amid those fragrant, colorful, astonishing vistas. Henry and Roper traveled over half the planet to gather ever more and rarer plants that would flourish in the mild, moist climate of Donegal and by the time they'd finished they had created one of the most remarkable gardens in the Western world. Like the collection in Philadelphia, it attracted crowds, buses filled with people prepared to travel to that extremely out-of-the-way corner of Ireland in order to admire the horticultural miracle. And there was the deer park, too. A sizable portion of Henry's 32,000 acres was set aside for the six or seven hundred deer that stamped majestically across the mountainsides, dissuaded from running away by twenty-eight miles of fence that had to be kept in good repair. During later years, the lord of all this splendor permitted visitors to come and stroll around one day every week when he was in residence, but they were never invited into the castle, lest they disturb Greta Garbo's solitary absorption in *The Golden Bowl.*

The guests were nearly numberless, though somewhere the Glenveagh guest books must survive and a patient researcher could probably compute the total, as Henry was punctilious about having every departing guest leave behind his signature. There must have been thousands. Some, like Garbo, Menuhin, Stephen and Natasha Spender, Bruce Chatwin, Lord Dunsany, Kenneth Clark et al., were excellent company. Others were irreparably boring. It made little difference. Henry could keep boredom pleasantly in abeyance with cascades of entertaining conversation, and often the entertainment came more from his witty manner than from his subject matter. It was both amusing and amazing to observe the ease with which he overcame conversational doldrums. His virtuosity and ingenuity as a host were unique. The raison d'être of Glenveagh, of course, and to a lesser extent of 1914, was to receive guests. I wouldn't say without reserve that it was Henry's own raison d'être, but this intimation might in later years have become credible.

In Athens, in the meantime, Aleco was in low spirits. Having finished his military service, he found himself at very loose ends. News of his dejection was not slow to reach Henry, and by a flutter of fate similar to that which had led the young fellow to make his way toward the gleaming yacht (with happier consequences than for James Gatz), it so happened that Henry was in a position to help. And he relished helping. A man with whom he had long before been intimate had become the assistant to the British filmmaker Tony Richardson, who was even then preparing to shoot a film in Greece. Henry wrote to his friend, asking whether some small part might be found, or created, for

Aleco in this production. If accommodating at all, the movie world can be made almost infinitely accommodating, and Aleco promptly found himself employed in the realm of make-believe. The star of the film—a flop, incidentally, but no matter—was a famed French actress, who had created a sensation some years before in a picture which featured scenes of sexual intercourse deemed very daring for that day. Not conventionally beautiful but with a vibrant personality, this actress was a star of international brilliance, temperamental and accustomed to satisfaction of her whims. The moment she laid eyes on Aleco, her whim dictated that he play the lead in her life, if not in the film. He was anything but averse, and their affair presently became a staple of gossip columns and trashy magazines like *Paris Match*, which published photos of the amorous couple. When filming was finished, Aleco was invited to accompany his lady love back to Paris. He accepted with even greater, and more understandable, enthusiasm than had led him years before to Glenveagh, New York, and Philadelphia. The actress had been married, had, in fact, a son aged about fifteen, and was known to have carried on numerous casual affairs. With Aleco, however, nothing was casual. Appreciably older than he, she conducted with genuine passion her relationship with this lusty, handsome, vivacious, and brightly sophisticated young man. Lessons learned from Henry proved to be expedient and effective. Whether she was aware of Aleco's erstwhile attraction to the yacht and the intimate consequences thereof we do not know, but in the movie milieu sexual reality was, and is, subject to the magic of make-believe, so she wouldn't have been perturbed by the ghost of a homosexual dalliance. Only present performance mattered, and Aleco was outstanding in the role assigned by happenstance. The scenario became serious. There was talk of marriage. This inevitably got into the papers. A date was set. But then, as in any self-respecting scenario, obstacles on the road to happiness directed it toward a dead end. The actress's son turned out to be an exceedingly headstrong teenager and was furiously opposed to the prospect of his mother's marriage to a man whom he regarded with loathing as a sidewalk species of gigolo. This was egregiously unfair to Aleco, but intemperate and insecure adolescents are unlikely to be well acquainted with disinterested cogitation. With sly duplicity, however, they can be on the best of terms, and instead of openly defying his mother, the son won over to his view the decisive verdict of the family lawyer. Marriage plans went down the drain. Aleco, smarting from what can only have seemed a second rejection—and the loss of what had appeared to promise a finer future than the past—had no choice but to return to Athens bearing the stigma of a public humiliation. I happened to be there on my way to an island paradise (now lost) and we had dinner together. The poor fellow was very deep down on his luck. His good looks were as spectacular as ever, but it is a sad fact that many more handsome men exist on earth than there are opportunities for them to gain lifelong advantage from transient physical allure.

Luck had twice been lavish with Aleco. To expect that a third stroke might come along would have seemed, to say the least, wishful. But it did, and it was the most lavish of all. It came about indirectly through Henry's intervention, demonstrating yet again that he possessed not only a horde but also a heart of gold.

In that summer of Aleco's deepest discontent Mrs. X was, if possible, even more distraught. And her reasons were not unlike his, though she probably felt that fate had naturally singled her out for an unkindness of exceptional distinction. She had, after all, been born in a palace, was the daughter of a duke, one of England's foremost, and would hardly have considered her destiny comparable to that of a common mortal. Mrs. X's noble father resided in one of the largest, ugliest piles in Great Britain, and he had named his daughter in memory of a famous forebear, the first duchess and all-powerful confidante of royalty. The young woman had become acquainted during World War II

with an American banker from Philadelphia, and they were married in 1943. Inevitably, she became friendly with Henry along
with all the rest of the local high society. Four daughters were
born and during a couple of decades all seemed tolerably well
with that ménage. But the duke's daughter was a restless and
foolish woman. How she came to encounter a character as dubious and shallow as X, I have no idea. They were not, to put
it mildly, of the same milieu, but he was strikingly handsome in
the Latin manner, attractive both to men and to women, with
a decided preference for the former. She fell for him, and he
was shrewd enough to recognize a good thing when it came
along. After all, she was not only the daughter of a duke but
the granddaughter of one of America's most famous heiresses,
unhappy wife to the seventh duke. So there was a very handsome
heritage when the grand old lady died. X's suit was therefore
excited by extravagant expectations, while the object of it was
beguiled by velvet talk, torrid youth, and skillful passion. Only
forty-five at the time, she felt she could afford a second, more
delightful lifetime. Henry did not approve of this affair, feeling
that a duke's daughter was looking for disillusionment by seek-
ing satisfaction where conditioning should have taught that it's
folly to take a chance. But he knew her to be willful as well as
foolish, and he was far too considerate to meddle with others'
emotions. Consequently, she hastened to become Mrs. X,
though she was never averse to being addressed as M'lady. The
misalliance promptly turned out to be a misfortune. As a lover
X must have been persuasive. As a husband he was odious, un-
faithful, mercenary. M'lady's friends disliked him, her daughters
hated him. There were quarrels, of which the sordid side was
no secret, and another divorce was soon imminent. The rapidity
of the marital débâcle was humiliating. She grew despondent.
The imbroglio was entirely of her own making, and for this
reason, perhaps, Henry felt more compassion for her than if she
had been the victim of an accident.

Despite the recent Six-Day War between Israel and its Arab

neighbors and the general tinderbox potential of the Middle East, Henry decided once again in that summer of 1967 to cruise in the Greek Isles. He invited the unhappy former Mrs. X to come along, and she gratefully accepted. Generously remembering another crestfallen victim of amorous misadventure, he also invited Aleco to join the cruise. Later he swore that he had never anticipated that for either of his dejected guests their meeting might lead to a renewed prospect of enduring and passionate bliss. A couple of the others aboard had been present when Aleco had first risen from the waters of Hydra harbor, and for them, as for Henry, what happened during this second cruise, considering the past history of both individuals, might have appeared promising material for a treacly novel by Mrs. Cartland. And yet, albeit both were on the rebound, there seemed no reason to doubt that M'lady and Aleco had truly fallen in love before the cruise was over. Aleco had been taught a lot by Henry. He knew that no actress possessed entrée to the delights of the great world comparable to a duke's daughter. As for M'lady, she saw that Aleco was a great improvement over X. He could very nearly pass for a gentleman, he was able to talk about Cézanne or Stravinsky, and it even seemed thinkable that he could be presented at the ducal palace, which was the next thing to Buckingham Palace itself. Besides, to make matters simpler, they were sincerely in love, and proved it by marrying before the end of the year. Henry happily made sure the arrangements were suitable. It was a stormy marriage, of course, but a marriage that endured. For a time. They built a large house near Corinth and filled it with the famous grandmother's Louis XVI furniture. And so Aleco drifted more or less out of Henry's life for good. And what a sum of good he'd garnered from having swum into it! Aleco and M'lady eventually separated—without too much acrimony, it seems—but Henry remained on the best of terms with both.

Something changed for Henry as he reached the age of sixty.

For forty years he had devoted his intellectual and material resources almost wholly to the study, appreciation, and acquisition
of works of art created between the beginning of the nineteenth
century and the first quarter of the twentieth. Although he had
denied himself few pleasures, this pursuit had been the pivot of
his life, the source of greatest satisfaction, and the guarantee that
he had kept up with his youthful aspirations and the uncompromising standards of Professor Sachs. His collection numbered
only about fifty works, of which almost half were drawings, but
each one represented the artist at his very best. Each had been
chosen with painstaking discrimination. Each had something
unique and memorable to say about the man who had created
it. And the roster of greatness was nearly overpowering: David,
Ingres, Delacroix, Corot, Degas, Chassériau, van Gogh, Cézanne, Matisse, Picasso. Monet and Gauguin were deliberately
omitted because Henry cared little for landscapes, possessing
only *Rain* as an example of this genre; he also disliked exotic
subject matter, but regretted the absence of Géricault and Manet. Among so many masterpieces it was not easy to designate
the greatest. Henry thought it was the David, but of course
Cézanne is by far the greater artist, and Henry's portrait of a
melancholy Madame Cézanne in a striped blouse, her hair un-
done and head tilted to the left, is equal in grandeur of concep-
tion, finesse of execution, and depth of emotion to many a
Rembrandt. It is not a beguiling picture, however, nor one easy
to live with. Among the most exquisite and delightful paintings
in the collection was Seurat's *The Models*, a small, late version of
his final, most complex and studied work, the large *Models*,
which hangs in the foundation of the odious Dr. Barnes amid
some seventy Cézannes, scores of Matisses, Picassos, Rousseaus,
a lot of messy Soutines, and more than a hundred Renoirs, every
last one of them mediocre, in suburban Merion, not twenty
miles from Rittenhouse Square. Painted in tiny pinpoints of
color, both versions of *The Models*, depicting three nude women

in varied poses in the artist's studio, are marvels of pointillism, the technique invented by Seurat. Henry and the hateful doctor were not, to put it politely, companionable, but Henry nonetheless took account of the contents of the Barnes Foundation when considering the fate of his own collection because he remained ever mindful of the cultural needs and resources of the larger Philadelphia area.

Because Henry's *Models* was so wonderfully sweet without being sentimental, so delicate and endearing, his decision to sell it at auction came as a startling shock to his friends. Christie's had promised him at least a million, which was still an exciting sum of money in those pre-Reagan days. But the great question was "Why?" The answer came frankly: "The trusts, my dear, the trusts!" He had been able in extremis to invade one or two, but now the bankers were inflexible. All remaining capital must be kept inviolate until his death. And living as Henry did had become more and more expensive. He groaned over the expense of Glenveagh, which now cost him in yearly upkeep ten times what he had paid for the entire estate three decades before. Then there were the cruises, the travels, the gifts, the servants, and the parties. Oh, the parties, the parties. Henry did adore giving parties, and nobody gave better ones. His greatest pleasure, I think, was to contrive that others should share in his own, nor was there anything even slightly ostentatious or vain about this career as a provider of good times. The host often seemed to be the most joyful and fortunate of the guests. And the ingenuity devoted to the variety of parties would have exhausted all but the most gregarious and convivial of social luminaries. These festivities varied from decorous Sunday afternoons for thirty to hear Fischer-Dieskau sing or Yehudi play the violin, to balls for a hundred and fifty, which sometimes grew hectic toward 3 a.m., to the occasional, hilarious fest for gentlemen only. Invitations to Henry's parties were prized as no others in Philadelphia, and he realized as well as anybody else that he had become the premier social arbiter of the city. All this fun, of which the pace grew more dashing as Henry grew older, cost money, and the host was resolved not to spare expense, never having had to, and determined not to start when common sense said that, whereas his collection might enjoy immortality, he was unlikely to share it. His health was good, but he took poor care of himself, ate and drank too much, and grew increasingly fat. The doctors told him that excess weight was the enemy of longevity, but he couldn't resist the fabulous food prepared by chefs paid accordingly.

It was nonsense, of course, to suggest that Henry was compelled to part with his Seurat in order to keep the wolf from the door. He could easily have initiated economies, entertained a little less frequently and sumptuously, or, if intent upon raising a handsome sum, sold his two Dalís and two Picassos, works he did not prize, plus some of the gold snuffboxes and rare silver gilt of which he possessed a large quantity. He need not have deprived his collection of one of its finest, rarest, most lovely ornaments. But economy was the very last practice Henry felt disposed to pursue. And he was determined to sell the Seurat, assuring by a single transaction the gain of a substantial sum. His determination, however, signified something more profound and troubling than a mere desire for money. By amputating this precious part of his collection, it seemed, he was betraying the presiding convictions of his lifetime. Was it conceivable that this was simply for the purpose of entertaining more guests and giving more splendid parties? And if so, what did this mean in terms of the true motivation of a committed collector? Only Henry could have guessed at an answer to such a complex question.

His decision to sell the Seurat is intriguing, perhaps, because it was not his first choice of a work by the painter. What he had really wanted was a large painting called *The Parade*, one of the six large pictures executed before the artist's death at age thirty-

one. It is a static, somber work, more important by virtue of
size, perhaps, but not nearly so beautiful as *The Models*. But it
would have made a stunning pendant to the Toulouse-Lautrec.
It had been in the stock of Knoedler's, the venerable New York
firm, the price $35,000. This was in the early thirties, the depth
of the Great Depression. Henry persuaded his mother to come
to New York, and Knoedler's sent the painting to her suite in
the Hotel St. Regis, while the firm's representative, a distinguished gentleman named Carmine Messmore, waited downstairs in the lobby. All afternoon Henry attempted to prevail on
his mother to buy the picture. But she wouldn't. She wanted to
spend the same amount on a fabulous Oriental carpet, because
her husband had loved them, to be given to the museum as the
major item of his collection, an example reputed to be one of
the finest sixteenth-century imperial rugs in existence, but which
later—too late—turned out to be a nineteenth-century imita-
tion.

The smaller, less expensive, less imposing, but far more beautiful *Models* was purchased later. It would be idle surmise, I
think, to fancy that Henry's decision to sell the Seurat was at all
influenced by pique at having missed the more imposing one he
wanted. But the coincidence is there. In the library at 1914 on
a table to the left of the fireplace had always stood a photograph
in a silver frame of Frances McIlhenny taken by George Platt
Lynes a few years before her death. She was visibly a lady of
strong will, principle, and personality. The photograph disappeared about the same time as the Seurat.

I knew a good deal about buying and selling pictures. From
a very early age I had haunted art galleries as well as museums,
even daring to visit before the age of twenty the awesome premises of Duveen Brothers, where I was received with exquisite
courtesy by a gentleman in a morning coat who showed me
drawings by Leonardo da Vinci. And I had occasionally accompanied Henry on visits to Wildenstein's, Knoedler's, and J. K.

Tannhauser's during his sojourns in New York. So it did not seem out of order for me to talk to him about the disposal of the Seurat. I advised against auction sale, certain that he could do far better, if less precipitously, by discreet private sale. It was no secret that the Rockefellers, Mellons, and Whitneys were never seen in the salesrooms, shy of the publicity attached to record-breaking prices, though when masterpieces were at stake they sometimes commissioned dealers to bid for them. But Henry had committed himself to Christie's through the intercession of a mutual friend. Besides, he felt that the prestige of his name would add to the picture's value, and he quite liked the attendant publicity. It was rather as though by selling the painting he was proving his discrimination more conclusively than he had by acquiring it in the first place. At all events, the sale took place and the result was rather disappointing. The price was nine hundred and some odd thousands of dollars, not near what Henry had hoped. The ready cash nevertheless came in handy.

1914 had begun to seem a bit cramped. There were only four guest rooms. The dining room could not comfortably accommodate more than about thirty people, and for a ball he was obliged to cover the garden with a tent and put down a highly polished floor to dance upon. Having bought and demolished the ugly, two-story house overlooking his garden, Henry in 1972 acquired the house on the other side of 1914, this one a tall, five-story stone mansion which would provide not only more guest rooms, a new office for his secretary, and living quarters for the butler, but also a space for an addition that Henry had long dreamed of: a ballroom. Here he would be able at last to give the grandest parties of his grand career as a giver of parties. The ballroom occupied the entire ground floor of the renovated mansion. As a space conceived entirely for the sake of entertainment and an example of what might be called Henry's "late" style, it was palatial, with much marble of various colors, crystal chandeliers, plenty of gilt bronze, and Doric columns. It was, to be blunt, rather ostentatious, but that, after all, was what was wanted in the only ballroom to be built in America after World War II. Henry was delighted. He was, indeed, proud, and the parties given in that ballroom, with music provided by an orchestra in the adjoining winter garden, seemed made to order, as they were, to justify delight and pride.

So life went on for Henry in a style which was, in fact, a remembrance of things past. Occasionally he acquired a work of art, most notably a superb van Gogh drawing of the Arles period, exchanged for the little Dalí painting he had picked up forty years before. He bought furniture, silver, snuffboxes. And he gave parties. He invited to Glenveagh guests whom he scarcely knew, especially if they happened to be handsome young men. And he was infallibly gracious to everyone even under circumstances that might reasonably have tried his patience. I recall with uncomfortable clarity a weekend in Philadelphia when I was the only guest in the house and one evening for dinner we were joined by one of Henry's nephews—I didn't bother to note which of Bonnie's four boys he was—a young man of superb self-esteem and crushing ennui, interested in absolutely nothing that could interest a person of mediocre cultivation. Though with nothing to say, he loved to talk and droned tediously through drinks and dinner. Afterwards we sat in the drawing room beneath the haughty gaze of the *Countess de Tournon* by Ingres and young Wintersteen went on talking. Maybe in the midst of his witless chatter he mused upon the prospect of the great good fortune that would be his when his uncle died. On and on and on he talked, with no intelligible point or purpose to so much tactless loquacity. I grew almost unbearably restive, thinking that Henry would certainly contrive some pretext for ridding us of the mortally monotonous nephew. But no. On the contrary, he was the very ideal of vivid courtesy, listening as if to Kenneth Clark talking about Turner, and responded with considered thought to the vapid ramblings of the idiotic young man. As the evening wore on and on, I wondered how long Henry could keep up the gracious pose of politeness. And it occurred to me that the nephew may have mused with regret upon the mountain of money (represented by the works of art) he would not inherit, but I doubted at the same time whether he ever suspected that in addition to cash he might have enjoyed an avuncular legacy that was priceless. It was after midnight before he finally got up to depart, and Henry bid him good night as if with genuine regret. When the front door closed behind him, I heaved a great sigh and suggested we have a last drink. Henry feelingly agreed. I asked him how he had been able to endure with impeccable courtesy so much tedium when it would have been easy to get rid of the nephew at least two hours earlier. I've never forgotten his response. "Well, my dear," he said, "I'll tell you. I learned long ago that a bore is only boring if you expect him to be like yourself. If you observe him with the same attention you would give to a strange work of art, you always have something to learn. So I consider the evening reasonably well spent, don't you see?" It might, I thought, have been a character from Henry James saying, "Live all you can; it's a mistake not to. It doesn't so much matter what you do in particular so long as you have your life." I like to believe that that evening I, too, learned something. The memory, in any case, remains intense, instructive, and seems to reveal something important about Henry.

Glenveagh as the years wore on had come to seem more and more like a gigantic pebble in one of Henry's shoes, a source of growing annoyance rather than of continued pleasure. Prices—and salaries!—in Ireland had risen and risen, while expenses multiplied. He had installed electricity and a telephone, having the cables buried at great cost so as not to mar the gardens with unsightly poles. The castle gradually came to seem like an implacable white elephant dragging its owner helplessly to his doom. He complained that the place was worthless, unsalable, and, to prove his point, even had a team of geologists come to make a survey in case precious resources lay hidden underground. They drilled and drilled but found only granite. It grew vexing to think how much money had been poured into a vast estate upon which rain fell steadily most of the year, which yielded only peat to burn in the castle's many fireplaces, masses of flowers from the great gardens, and trout for those patient enough to fish in the lake. What person in his right mind would want to purchase such an enormous property, including the herd of seven hundred deer, for a price even remotely related to its cost? The apparent answer became increasingly exasperating. But then, to the astonishment of everyone concerned, the remarkable value of Glenveagh seemed suddenly as transparent as a pane of glass, and the ruthless policy of land clearing which had cost Black Adair his life a century before would pay at last a handsome dividend. It's odd that nobody had seen the potentiality before. The simple fact was that, with the passing of time and the rising costs of nearly everything, Glenveagh had become by far the largest privately owned parcel of land in all the Republic of Ireland. Moreover, the vast, expensive gardens and enormous deer park were added attractions. The government conveyed expressions of interest with a view to making a public park and wildlife sanctuary of the Glenveagh Castle Estate. They were prepared to pay, and to pay handsomely. Henry was ecstatic. He had now passed his seventieth birthday, celebrated in Philadelphia in May of 1976 with a party as good as one of his own, and the chilly, rainy summers at Glenveagh no longer delighted him as once they had. There was some haggling over the price, which was finally set at three million dollars. Friends expected that Henry would be sad to leave Glenveagh, which by now had become so much his own creation, that he would miss the moors and bogs, the gardens, the deer park, the hideous but comfortable castle itself, even the rain. Not at all. He was delighted.

Henceforth he would spend his summers, and a part of each winter, in exceedingly luxurious rented villas and mansions in warm climates. In Italy, Hawaii, Austria, South America, Florida, where he knew lots of people and could go on giving wonderful parties and receiving illustrious, entertaining guests.

In the same year that he left Glenveagh, Henry once more surprised his friends by selling another of the most beautiful paintings in his collection. Why he felt disposed to do so after the lucrative Irish transaction seemed incomprehensible. Maybe after the years of financial caution imposed by the maternal trusts he simply wanted to have sufficient cash on hand to do exactly as he pleased and buy works of art if he felt like it, though he bought only one or two drawings. In any case, when he made up his mind to sell something, he chose one of the very finest works in his collection, one not so rare as the Seurat but a first-rate painting by a greater artist, Paul Cézanne. It was a still life of a white sugar bowl with blue drapery and pears, apples, and a lemon on a table, a serene, deeply moving work of the artist's finest period, painted in the early nineties. It had always hung above the dining-room fireplace at 1914. Henry had attempted to explain away the sale of the Seurat by saying that the large version was visible in nearby Merion, and he now said that the Philadelphia area had plenty of still lifes by Cézanne. The rationalization is not entirely convincing for the simple reason that Henry had not formed his collection primarily for the pleasure or benefit of the citizens of Philadelphia. It had been his private creation, his intimate raison d'être, the love of his life, one might say, and his willingness to diminish again its beauty and importance by selling one of the very best pictures seems to entail a perplexing denial of the self. And yet Henry was too intelligent and too sensitive to betray the zeal and quest of a lifetime. There is the mystery. Its solution can hardly be sought in a frivolous desire to give grand parties and live in ostentatious splendor. So there is a mystery within the mystery, and perhaps it was this that added to Henry's personality that aura of rare but remote charm which made his company uniquely agreeable and challenging. The Cézanne, in any case, got sold, like the Seurat, at Christie's, where it fetched about the same amount as Glenveagh Castle.

Henry spent the month of September 1984 in Venice, where he rented a lovely villa set amid surprising, spacious gardens on the Giudecca. Although he had continued his annual "cure" at Montecatini, it did him not an ounce of good, for he had by this time grown well beyond being fat and was frankly obese. He ate with as zestful an appetite as ever and said, "What does it matter, my dear? Nobody sees me naked except Patrick and he's hardened to the spectacle." Accompanied by my companion and adopted son Gilles Roy, plus a couple of our pals, I was also in Venice that September, having rented an apartment for the first week of the month in the Palazzo Corner Spinelli, large but late, on the Grand Canal. We saw Henry almost every day. Having prudently brought with him his butler, his chef, and a footman, he gave a formal luncheon on the third, among the guests the Duchess of Westminster, Paloma Picasso, and the masterly biographer of her father, John Richardson. Two days later he was present at a large cocktail party. On the seventh he gave another luncheon and in the late afternoon attended a cocktail party at the splendid Palazzo Barbaro, a home made famous by Henry James, often a guest there, as the fictional residence of Milly Theale, heroine of *The Wings of the Dove*. The hostess was Baroness Franchetti, for years one of Venice's most eminent hostesses. She had fallen on hard times, however, due to the folly of her husband, who ran through her fortune and sullenly refused to appear at her parties. In order to make of this party the sort of festivity to which he himself was accustomed, but which the unhappy baroness could no longer afford, Henry sent over from the Giudecca his butler, a footman, champagne, liquor, and caviar sandwiches. Later we went on to another party, at the truly palatial palace of Alessandro Albrizzi, a warm-hearted nobleman of antique lineage. In one *salone* hung portraits of numerous forebears by Longhi. The ballroom was—and still is, I know, though Alessandro is no longer, alas, present to entertain there—a masterpiece of seventeenth-century rococo decoration. Afterwards we went for dinner almost inevitably to Harry's Bar. Henry had been eating and drinking all day long, but he was in the most ebullient of spirits. He invited me to visit him in Honolulu the following winter, but I was just then finishing my fifteen-year labor on the biography of Giacometti and doubted I could accept. "Oh well, my dear," he cried, "we're sure to meet again somewhere." If we do, I wonder where it will it be, because that was the last time I ever saw Henry.

He spent part of the winter of 1985 and 1986 in Honolulu, where he met or knew everybody, being on the best of terms with the Dillinghams, who reigned over the island society. He traveled a good deal, spent less time than usual in Philadelphia, and took guests along with him wherever he went. So it was that Alessandro Albrizzi happened to be in Honolulu in the early spring of 1986. It seemed to him that Henry was not as lively and high-spirited as usual. A kind and gentle person, Alessandro consequently took the trouble on his own initiative to communicate with Henry's doctor in Philadelphia and ask his advice. It was categorical. Henry should return home immediately for a thorough examination. All those decades of luxurious living had placed a severe strain on his heart, and it was possible that a complex coronary-bypass operation might be required. Though the term of the lease on Henry's estate had not yet expired, he obediently did as the doctor ordered. Examination in Philadelphia showed that, indeed, a serious operation was urgently needed. A date early in May was set, and then suddenly Bonnie Wintersteen died just two weeks before Henry was due to enter the hospital. He said, "How thoughtless of Bonnie to die just when I'm to have this serious operation." She had disappointed him, for her interest in art and dedication to the cultivated life had turned out to be superficial.

The necessary operation was performed but revealed that Henry's heart, which metaphorically had been so great and generous, was irreparably damaged. He died on May 12, 1986.

The pictures, the best furniture, the finest silver, the decorative objects all went, as he had always desired, to the Philadelphia Museum, which received in toto four hundred and fourteen objects, among which were six paintings that are by any criterion outstanding masterpieces of Western art: the David, the Ingres, *The Death of Sardanapalus* by Delacroix, the Degas *Interior*, *Madame Cézanne*, and the Toulouse-Lautrec. They form part of the Henry P. McIlhenny Collection, given in memory of Frances P. McIlhenny. So the love of his life was dedicated to the one who had given him life and had assisted him as long as she lived to seek and to find difficult and unique fulfillment on his own terms. Visitors to the museum who contemplate with emotion Henry's bequest will have no idea who he was or what he was like. A decade suffices to generate an immense measure of forgetfulness. But Henry would not lament. He was glad to give his life to great art and to find his life enhanced by it. If a visitor to the Philadelphia Museum of Art is occasionally clairvoyant enough to comprehend this rare raison d'être, Henry will never cease giving splendid parties.

Part Two

SUDBURY COTTAGE

ISABEL RAWSTHORNE

The very first time I heard her name was on Thursday, September 17, 1964. This was the fifth day I had been posing for a portrait by Alberto Giacometti. He had returned only six days previously from London, where he had gone to inspect the rooms set aside for a large retrospective exhibition of his work at the Tate Gallery the following year. His wife, Annette, had remained behind in England, going to spend a few days in the country with a woman named Isabel, with whom Alberto had been in love many years before. "A real devourer of men," he remarked. "A tigress. No. More like a panther." But she had changed his life, he added, for it had been because of her that he had found himself one night alone in the Place des Pyramides, where a car ran him down, crushing his foot, an event that transformed his existence and his work forever. Till the end of his days he walked with a slight limp.

Though I conscientiously noted Alberto's comment, Isabel's identity, even her role in his past life, meant nothing to me then. I was not curious enough to inquire about her further. Sixteen months afterwards Alberto was dead, and I had lost my chance to question the one person whose account would have had the most meaning. I never guessed at the time that the woman called Isabel would have a part to play in my posthumous relation to Alberto.

Meanwhile I learned a little. Isabel, née Nicholas, was married to a man named Rawsthorne, an English composer of mediocre accomplishment. She was a close friend of Francis Bacon, just then beginning to enjoy worldwide fame as the most prolific and controversial painter of the post-Picasso generation, and many of his tortured, dislocated figures were purported to be "portraits" of Isabel. Consequently, she was a personage of some stature in the world of contemporary art.

Then it suddenly became evident that I would need to learn more about Isabel and her relation to the art world of her era, because late in 1969 I rashly agreed to attempt to compose a biography of Giacometti. On Saturday, March 7, 1970, I went to London, where I already knew several people who I assumed would be well acquainted with Isabel, since they were also close friends of Francis Bacon. These were David Sylvester, the art critic, Erica Brausen, the dealer who had first exhibited Bacon's work and set him on the way to fame and wealth, and Véra Russell, first wife of John Russell, also an art critic. I was right. They were willing not only to talk frankly about Isabel's past life but to explain to me how to get in touch with her, since she spent most of her time in a cottage in a tiny town north of London in Essex.

Isabel would then have been close to sixty. She had been born in London, the daughter of an officer in the British merchant marine. As a child she saw little of him, since he was usually away at sea, and he died in some far-off land while she was still a girl. Her mother and a younger brother emigrated not very long afterwards to Canada, but Isabel determined to remain in England. Having shown exceptional talent for drawing while in school, she decided to become an artist and won a scholarship to the Royal Academy in London. Strikingly beautiful, she revealed something both exotic and dramatic in her appearance and personality. Life as a scholarship student in the thirties was not easy, and Isabel yearned for creative fulfillment and much enjoyment of life's pleasures. Therefore, indifferent to the prudish admonitions of her professors, she determined to seek work as an artist's model. Her face and figure made it easy to find. Before long, she had become the favorite model of the most noted sculptor in England, Jacob Epstein. He produced numerous effigies of her, and for him she produced a son. Now, Mrs. Epstein was phenomenally tolerant of her husband's easy way with models, but the child's birth exceeded her faculty for tolerance and she insisted upon keeping and rearing as her own the adulterous offspring. Epstein was compelled to humor this desire and persuaded the legitimate mother to do likewise. Isabel never saw her son again, and never bore another, but the privation transformed her life, because the apologetic father generously made it possible for her to set herself up in Paris, where no embarrassment might ensue, though everyone who knew them knew the truth. And it was in the germinal atmosphere of the Parisian art world of the mid-thirties that Isabel, not yet twenty-five and at the height of her dynamic beauty, came entirely into her own as a being to bewilder and vanquish men.

The first of them was a celebrated British journalist, Sefton Delmer, who promptly married her and established their home in a luxurious apartment conveniently near the Hotel Ritz. The young wife, however, had not forgotten her artistic ambitions, promptly found a studio, and soon became an *habituée* of the Left Bank cafés where artists congregated. Quick-witted and sociable, she learned French in a hurry and gave many hectic parties in the grand rooms overlooking the Place Vendôme. Alcohol flowed like an upland torrent, and it was then that Isabel began a lifelong love affair with drink. It was also then that she became acquainted with Giacometti. When the war broke out, she and her husband made a last-minute escape to London.

Through his influence she found a position in the intelligence service. Their marriage did not survive the hostilities. Afterwards she went back for a time to Paris, but returned to England and married a musician called Constant Lambert, who died of alcoholism four years later. Alan Rawsthorne was her next husband, he too a devotee of the bottle. They kept a *pied-à-terre* in London, but spent most of their time in a remote country cottage, where the husband could compose and the wife paint. Their telephone number there was Great Sampford 250. And that was all that I knew about Isabel before meeting her.

Tuesday afternoon March 10, I called Great Sampford. The answer was so prompt that I imagined the telephone must have been immediately at hand. A woman's voice, throaty and rich but peculiarly metallic, as if the voice box were made of copper. It was Mrs. Rawsthorne speaking, she said. I explained who I was, and that I wished to meet her to talk about Giacometti, of whom I might, I said, undertake to write a biography.

"Oh, I've heard of you," she said. "Alberto used to talk about you sometimes. 'My Yankee friend,' he used to say."

I tried to make clear to her that above all I wanted to cause no inconvenience.

"Well," she said, "I'm not a monster, you know."

"I didn't mean to suggest you might be," I protested.

"Some people think I am," she remarked, followed by a shriek of laughter that hurt my eardrum.

"So you just want to have a conversation about Alberto, is that it?"

"Yes, nothing more," I said, although there was, to be sure, much more. "I'm not going to give you the third degree."

She laughed again. "That's been tried," she said, "with little success. So if you just want to have a conversation, why don't you come up here the day after tomorrow? You can have dinner with me and my husband and stay overnight in a hotel nearby, a place called the Swan Hotel in Thaxted. And then we might meet again the next morning if we aren't talked to tatters. Would that suit you?"

"That would be perfect," I said.

She explained in detail how I should make my way toward her rural retreat, having a timetable beside her. I should take a train from the Liverpool Street Station at 6:36 p.m., getting off at Audley End, where she would meet me.

Anxious to make an ostentatious show of appreciation for such prompt hospitality, I went on Thursday afternoon to the flower department at Harrods, near where I was staying, and purchased a camellia bush in full bloom almost as tall as I was, both bulky and heavy. But I got it into a taxi and arrived at the station at six o'clock. Struggling with the large camellia and a small suitcase, I must have presented a bizarre spectacle in the station crowded with hurrying commuters. I managed to find a first-class compartment empty and seated myself by the window with the camellia completely blocking access to the seat opposite. The compartment soon filled up, however, and, despite glances of surprise, the other passengers made no comment or protest about the invasive plant, which occupied space enough for a very corpulent passenger. I was particularly embarrassed because two handsome young men were obliged to stand in the corridor outside. But most of the passengers got off at the first stop.

It was a dreary day, fields and hills the color of gunmetal, with patches of exhausted snow here and there in the hollows. After about an hour of rackety stopping and starting, we reached Audley End, where I was able to disembark with the camellia and my small suitcase barely before the train clanked away. I was the only passenger on the platform and the town did seem well named, a small, drab place set down for no apparent reason amid barren hills and dirty fields. I had to wait in the spiritless little station, where I noticed that the letterbox actually—and everything else spiritually—had "VR" embossed upon it.

After about twenty minutes, when I was starting to wonder
whether I'd been forgotten, an antiquated automobile pulled up
in front. A woman got out. My first impression of her was all
gray. She seemed a little hesitant coming toward me, but as I
was the sole person present I could only have been the one
expected. Holding forward her hand, she said, "James Lord,"
and as we shook she burst out laughing, a hoarse, half-strangled,
throaty, strained, but very infectious laugh, adding, "I presume."

"But this is not Lake Tanganyika," I replied, hoping to im-
press her by the affected rapidity of my *à propos.*

"You're bloody well right it isn't," she cried. "And I am Isabel Rawsthorne."

An elderly man was then getting out of the automobile. Assuming him to be Alan Rawsthorne, I held forward my hand,
which he shook with conspicuous diffidence, suggesting that I
put my bag into the boot. I brought forward the camellia, by
which Isabel was satisfactorily impressed, even showing signs of
genuine pleasure. Getting it into the rear of the automobile was
no easy trick, but we managed, and I sat beside it. Isabel sat in
front with the driver and we set off. By that time it was dark.

Isabel turned half-round to me from her seat and we spoke
casually of Alberto and Diego as we drove very slowly along.
She said she had always considered Diego the more determined
of the two brothers. She laughed frequently, one of the strangest
laughs I have ever known: very appealing in its loud spontaneity
and directness, simplicity and readiness of response, but too
ready at the same time, too insistent and demanding, taking one
for granted somehow, dismissing one and plowing one under—
all of which added to the half-mad, metallic timbre of it. The
strength of her personality was immediately definite, sharp as a
dagger, but also a performance, something one could stand away
from and consider—for one's safety, perhaps?—dissociated from
causes or consequences—yet a rare, singular state of being. It

filled up time and space like a natural element, water or air. Indeed, I was decidedly conscious of an exceptional presence, though mindful that one might need to exercise vigilance, remembering what Alberto had said. And yet . . . I was aware as well that I was witness to what must have been but a remnant, the worn, vitiated remains of something that had once been voracious and triumphant.

She asked where I was staying and I told her, remarking that in general I disliked staying in hotels. She said that in England hotels were considered an unpleasant necessity and that people stayed in them only when they had no alternative. But she had lived frequently in hotels abroad, she added, where they were acceptable, even agreeable, places of residence. I asked where in Paris she had resided. At first in a splendid apartment overlooking the Place Vendôme, being married then to a journalist who earned large fees. "And is that where you lived until the war began?" I inquired.

"Oh no," she exclaimed, laughing again, "my life history is much more complicated than that." The odor of alcohol was perceptible on her breath.

The man at the wheel said almost nothing except when we came to a turn or intersection, at which moments he seemed unsure of the way and Isabel directed him. I thought that strange. But at length she said, "Perhaps I should explain. This gentleman is a friendly taxi driver, but he hasn't driven very often in this direction."

After some forty-five minutes of slow and hesitant driving, approaching through a very narrow lane, we finally reached a long, low, thatched cottage, Isabel's home. I got the camellia plant out of the car and carried it inside, remarking, "I'm glad to have gotten this tree safely to its destination."

"It will be happy here," said Isabel. "I love camellias and I know just the spot for it. How kind of you to have taken the trouble to carry such a bulky shrub all this way. But of course," she added, laughing, "you wanted to make a good impression on the lady with secrets you hope to worm out."

"Quite true," I admitted. Candor was clearly the path to pursue with Isabel.

Alan Rawsthorne was inside. He stood for our introduction. A man of medium height, half bald, with a very red face and a large paunch, a slow-moving, bland, sociable person, he must have been well over sixty. He did not remain standing for long.

The taxi driver came in with my bag and was invited to stay for a drink. His name proved to be Regan, which provided Alan with the opportunity to make some witticism about Goneril, leaving the driver utterly at a loss as we laughed. He said, "Oh, the name's familiar to you, is it?" And we replied that, indeed, it was.

While my hosts were occupied with the taxi driver, who was to come back later and take me to my hotel, I had an opportunity to inspect the interior of the cottage. It was frankly shabby. Just inside the doorway stood two very dilapidated over-stuffed armchairs in front of a large fireplace in which a few logs smoldered, giving off little warmth. From one of the chairs the stuffing drooped out in several places, and the ugly, wine-colored upholstered was shiny with grease and stains. The other was equally ugly but not quite so worn and filthy. There was also a high, uncomfortable-looking wooden chair. The ceiling was low, with dark rafters. The place could have been made charming and cozy, but there had obviously been no care taken for pleasing appearance, and I assumed that such considerations would have been deemed almost philistine to the proprietors. Propped on a bookcase at the back of the room was one of the finest portraits of Diego by Alberto I'd ever seen, but framed in an ugly silver molding. There were two small paintings by Bacon in a single, very elegant gilt frame, portraits, I supposed, of Isabel. On top of a large, ungainly Jacobean sideboard was a bronze bust of Isabel by Alberto, a work from the thirties. There were a couple of busts of Rawsthorne, too, good likenesses but not the work of an original hand. On the wall by the door onto a veranda hung a large, gray-green, dark landscape which I assumed to be by Isabel. It reminded me just a little, oddly enough, of Dora Maar's painting, romantic and lyrical but undisciplined, subjective, self-indulgent.

After the departure of the taxi driver, we sat down in front of the fire to drink, Rawsthorne occupying the wooden chair. He was drinking red wine and obviously had consumed a good deal of it already. Isabel had vermouth, I Scotch. There were a couple of cats, which accounted in part no doubt for the devastated furniture. Since the hotel where I was to stay did not serve dinner at this time of year, Isabel explained, we would dine at the cottage. I apologized for the inconvenience, but she did not seem to mind. The talk was quick, amusing, gossipy. Intelligence, I presumed, was so easily taken for granted that no one felt any need to invent intelligent conversation.

At one moment Isabel remarked that, in fact, they knew nothing whatever about me, so I said, "I'll tell you all about myself if you like."

She immediately rejoined, "Well, I won't do as much!" and burst out laughing. She was as good as her word.

Several times she went out of the room to the kitchen, and once while she was gone Alan said, "You knew Alberto."

"Yes," I said, "pretty well. And so did you, I suppose."

"I saw him a few times when he was in London for his exhibitions, that's all. But Isabel knew him very well."

There was plenty, and more than enough, to drink before dinner. At one moment, while Isabel was out of the room, Alan poured himself yet another glass of wine, and I sat staring in silence at the fire, feeling that in consideration of his compulsive taste for alcohol the sound of the pouring wine was as embarrassing as if he'd been urinating in a corner of the room. His wife could be heard talking in the kitchen. "Talking to the cats," I remarked.

"To herself more likely," said Alan. "Sometimes when I'm

working upstairs I hear entire conversations down here, and it's simply Isabel talking to herself. But of course, when you think of the life she's lived, she's got plenty to talk about."

The dining room was a glass-enclosed veranda, a very ugly space, roofed over with hideous blue-green corrugated plastic. But the dinner was excellent: celery soup, cold ham, and roast beef, Dauphinois potatoes, salad, and cheese, all accompanied by much Beaujolais. At one moment, the bottle being empty, I timidly inquired whether there might be more. Isabel laughed and said, "The wine *flows* in this house." While we ate, seated next to her on a sponge-rubber banquette in an awkward brick alcove, I was able to observe Isabel more closely. I noticed especially her hands, which were heavy, coarse, cracked, and dirty, almost deformed in contrast to the remaining finesse of her features. Also I could see that her eyes, which were rather prominent, were red, watery, and so glazed that it seemed almost as though a film of some very thin plastic had been drawn across them. I couldn't help thinking of the numerous portraits Bacon had painted of her, and because of the strange resemblance, despite the violence, the savagery, in fact, of their deformation, it occurred to me to wonder just what it was that that homosexual artist saw in this ruined and degraded beauty. Notwithstanding her intelligence, humor, and vibrant personality, I thought, could it be precisely because she was no longer beautiful, no longer young and triumphant as a woman, that Bacon was drawn to her? This wreck of victorious womanhood, this ruin of female allure: could that have been what appealed to Bacon? A curious question. It reminded me of the question Bacon had once asked of Alberto, who repeated it to me: "Do you believe it possible for a homosexual to be a great artist?" Alberto indignantly insisted that it was. I couldn't help thinking, nevertheless, that the deformations of women in Alberto's own art—not to mention Picasso's—were fundamentally and aesthetically very unlike those of Bacon.

As the dinner progressed, the talk became more ribald and loud and drunken. Isabel pounded on the table to emphasize her remarks, while Alan grew vaguer and vaguer. I felt at moments exceedingly awkward, as if I were surreptitiously observing a scene which the participants would not have wanted any outsider to witness. Still, they went on drinking, talking, and laughing. Once, when Isabel had gone to the kitchen and Alan to the living room in search of a cigarette, leaving me all alone for a moment, I stared into the distance and whispered aloud, "Help!" And yet I was amused. Toward the end of the meal Isabel had become so drunk that she could no longer eat properly. She had food all over her hands, and there were no napkins. It was highly embarrassing, but neither she nor Alan seemed to notice.

Isabel suggested that we have cheese in the living room in front of the fire, which we did, scattering crumbs across the floor. The talk continued loud and easy. At one moment Alan suggested that he might retire so that Isabel and I could talk, but she insisted that he stay, adding, "We can talk tomorrow." So the conversation went wildly on until there came a sudden knock at the door which made us all, including the cats, jump. It was only the taxi driver come to drive me to the hotel. Isabel said at the door, "Call me tomorrow morning at eleven."

"But you haven't done any talking at all," said Alan, meaning that the only mention of Alberto throughout the entire evening had come from him.

"Oh, but the time hasn't been lost," cried Isabel. "Not at all. The time has been very well spent."

I optimistically took this to mean that a rapport of some confidence had been established, which might later lead to information useful for my work. It was calculating, but a conscientious biographer must steel himself to be cunning, if not unscrupulous. And I honestly agreed with Carlyle's assertion that biography is by nature the most universally profitable, universally pleasant of all writing. But the subject must be a great man. Alberto was.

I agreed to call in the morning, made effusive thanks for my hosts' hospitality, and went out to the taxi.

Driving through the invisible, unknown countryside, I couldn't help thinking it strange that Alberto four years after his death had brought me here to this foreign land to meet the extraordinary, moving, drunken woman he had once loved. I felt her loss, the past yawning behind her in the dark absence of those she had once loved and who long ago had loved her. She had said that her life history had been complicated, but I sensed that in the very complication dwelt still a certain grandeur and it was then the thought came to me that I might someday try to take the measure of it.

The Swan Hotel was nondescript and careworn, the electric fire inadequate against chill and damp. Thaxted is a pleasant, uninteresting village with a very fine, exceptionally large early Gothic church. I called Isabel at eleven-fifteen. She suggested that I arrange for Mr. Regan to drive me there at about two-thirty, then call for me again at six o'clock to take me to Audley End, where I could catch a train back to London. And she added that three hours was the most she could spend with me, because after that she would become vague.

When I arrived at the cottage, I found that daylight did not render it either charming or picturesque, only accentuating the urgent need for repair. On the other side of the road stood a complex of very ugly modern sheds and farm buildings, while across the field marched high-tension pylons in a hideous file.

Isabel and Alan were in the dining veranda just then, preparing to have lunch, which consisted of leftovers from the previous evening. A bottle of Beaujolais was already half empty. The view across the barren fields was immersed in fog. I sat while they ate. By daylight Isabel appeared less lined and wrinkled than at night, her hands not actually deformed but coarse and dirty. She was not drunk, which may have affected my impression. Alan appeared no different save that his fleshy nose looked even more livid by day.

During lunch Isabel spoke of her past, her parents and younger brother, Warwick. Her father died when she was fifteen, but she had hardly known him, since he was so often absent at sea, and his family was mainly reminded of him by the strange wild animals he used to bring home from far-off places and leave behind as pets. No mention was made of the mother. We had coffee in the living room, occupying the places where we had sat the evening before. I was eager to have Alan leave us so we could begin our conversation, but he gave no sign of being in a hurry to go. The talk meandered aimlessly, with no mention of Alberto. I thought to give it a useful turn by referring to the bust of Isabel on top of the Jacobean cupboard. This did bring about a vague, very discursive conversation about Alberto and his work but between Isabel and Alan only. Mention was made of Derain, and I asked whether Isabel had known him. "Very well," she said. "There was a time when I saw him almost every day. I have a portrait of myself by him upstairs somewhere. I knew Picasso as well, knew them all, as a matter of fact."

A fresh bottle of wine had been opened to accompany our coffee. At last I was able to turn the conversation toward my concern. Isabel said she didn't think Annette or Diego would care what revelations came out. As for Alberto, she felt sure that he would be positively delighted to have every last detail related. I observed that Annette might not like to have much mention made of her husband's lifelong preoccupation with prostitutes. "Maybe," said Isabel, "that was more talk than action. Alberto did have problems, it's true, but he never let them dominate him."

I asked about the accident that had caused the injury to his foot and left him lame. At first Isabel seemed inclined to dismiss it, saying, "I wasn't there." But then she explained that Alberto had accompanied her to her hotel one night and that otherwise he would not have found himself on the spot where the accident had occurred. After a moment's hesitation she added, "Alberto always said the car that ran him down had been driven by a prostitute. I'm sure he thought that was the truth. He hated lying. But his imagination, you might say, had a will of its own."

I said nothing but felt suddenly that my trip had become valuable. Isabel went on to say that she had visited Alberto every day in the clinic where he was recuperating, took him books to read, and spent hours with him, laughing and gossiping. She spoke at some length about the exceptionally close relationship between Alberto and Diego, an old story to anyone who knew them.

Was it she, I inquired, who had introduced Alberto to Bacon? No. She had often spoken of one to the other but had had no opportunity to introduce them. Bacon was a great admirer of Alberto's work, happened to see him one day about 1960 in a café, and introduced himself. Then they became friends. When I said that I was eager to meet Bacon and talk to him about Alberto, Isabel quite spontaneously wrote down his address and phone number.

Alan's presence was disconcerting and irritating. Several times he said that he intended to leave us alone to talk but found the conversation so interesting that he preferred to stay. I suspected that the conversation interested him far less than the wine bottle, which continued to receive his close attention. The methodical but disorganized manner in which he spoke was maddening, as was the compulsive precision and deliberate puffing with which he lighted and smoked countless cigarettes. Both he and Isabel insisted that I have a whisky. I hate to drink during the day but could hardly decline, and one whisky turned out to be three.

Isabel offered to let me have copies of all the letters Alberto had written her. All except the indiscreet ones, she specified, laughing. The letters written during the war when he was working in a little hotel room in Geneva were the most interesting, she said, because that period had been his time of trial in the desert. Then there was a lot of aimless talk, helped in its irrelevance by the fact that all three of us were quite drunk. At a quarter of six the dependable taxi driver arrived. Both Isabel and Alan were very friendly and insisted that I must return in the spring or summer. I promised to do so, having not the least expectation or desire ever to see Sudbury Cottage again.

It was a breathtaking relief to escape from that oppressive place. I said not a word to Mr. Regan on our way to Audley End but gave him a large tip.

In the train on my way back to London I wrote in my journal and spent some time gazing out the window at the somber landscape, musing on the events of the past twenty-four hours. Certainly there was something phenomenal about Isabel, something unique and rather intimidating. What was it? An apparent, defiant determination to live life on her own terms absolutely. Her frequent metallic laughter reminded me of animal cries one might hear in the jungle at night. Not that I had ever been near a jungle. But there was that very strong sense of the wild. I remembered Alberto having said that she had been a devourer of men, a tigress or panther. Or a sphinx who did away with all those who could not answer her riddle. That seemed more like it. Perhaps Alberto had been able to answer it. There was the injured foot and the fact that his wife and mother bore the same name. Isabel, moreover, appeared to be concentrated on the proximity of the abyss. Her presence was threatening but at the same time captivating. I thought that she could very well cause havoc to reign. But there was more to it than that, perplexing and, yes, challenging. I felt confident we would meet again.

Little did I dream, however, that that meeting would occur barely more than a month later. On Friday, April 17, I was awakened by the telephone and the raucous voice of Isabel, laughing, of course. What could she possibly be doing up and around at that improbable hour, I wondered. She told me she had come over to Paris with Francis Bacon for only a day or two and would like to see me that very afternoon at six o'clock at the Hôtel des Saints-Pères. I agreed, of course, thinking hopefully that I might meet Bacon, too, who was high on my list of people to be interviewed.

Arriving at the hotel precisely at six, I asked at the desk for Madame Rawsthorne only to be told that she was out and would return later. So I went into the salon that faced the street. Two other people were seated there, a man and a woman, both middle-aged. I took a chair equidistant between them. The man I immediately recognized as Bacon. His dark blue shirt was very tight and the vents above his belly were so stretched that patches of white flesh showed through. A typically Bacon detail, I thought. The suit was brown and rumpled, while on his knees he held a suede coat bunched into a ball. We looked speculatively at each other for a minute or two, then Bacon said, "Are you waiting for Isabel?"

I said, "Yes."

"Then you must be James Lord."

"And you're Francis Bacon, aren't you?" I asked.

We shook hands and I moved to a chair closer to his. I told him at once that I'd been anxious to see him in order to talk about Giacometti, whose biography I planned to write. He said, "Well, I didn't really know him intimately. But I was very happy to see him in the last few years of his life, especially when he came to London in connection with the Tate show in 1965. I admired his frankness and intelligence more than anyone else I've ever known. Just exactly what are you planning to write?"

"Well, a biography," I said.

"Yes, but there are all sorts of biographies. And Alberto wasn't Queen Mary. I think the only decent sort of biography is one that tells everything, the really intimate account. Otherwise, it's just a scarecrow."

"I agree," I said. "But not everybody feels that way. How would you feel if someone wrote the full truth about you?"

"I wouldn't care," he replied. "But some of the people I've known would mind, and I'd mind their minding."

"What happens to the truth?" I said.

Bacon shrugged. "The truth is the shadow behind the shadow. Does it really matter? I mean, when millions of people are tortured and murdered, does it matter, after all, after the priests and the executioners have walked out hand in hand? The soul is a delusion. I don't believe in life after death, you know."

"Nor I," I said. "Did you feel intimidated by Alberto?"

"Never. I felt unusually at ease with him."

"Sometimes," I said, "I had the impression that he felt a kind of special sympathy or rapport with homosexuals, though he claimed he'd never had any experience."

"It's possible," Bacon said. "I had a lover called George, and once when Alberto was in London and we were riding in a taxi, he slapped George on the knee and said, 'When I'm in London, I feel homosexual.' I've thought sometimes that if Alberto had had a homosexual experience, it might have liberated something important in him. But I have lots of theories about Giacometti, and of course they're only theories." He added that Alberto's relations with women had, in any case, been unusual, and asked whether I thought Isabel had had a true affair with him; personally he doubted it, though he had never presumed to ask her. I said I didn't know.

We talked about Dubuffet, for whom Bacon had little respect. The conversation wandered on to Matisse and Picasso, about both of whom Bacon felt strong reservations, remarking that Picasso had done nothing of value since the early thirties, including *Guernica*. He asked if I'd like a drink. By that time we were on very easygoing terms. We both had whisky and continued chatting. I mentioned Mondrian and said I admired his efforts but didn't much like the outcome. Bacon replied that all-

—and he insisted on the *all*—abstract art was purely decorative, remarking, however, that he did not consider Cubism abstract.

After nearly an hour—and I was grateful for the delay—Isabel hurried in, out of breath, wearing dark glasses, which she did not take off, explaining apologetically that they were "necessary" today. That morning she had had a terrible hangover but apparently felt better, because she promptly ordered a Ricard. There was considerable talk about Sonia Orwell and Marguerite Duras, who had been great friends for years but now and then had furious quarrels. Isabel seemed nervous, pulling repeatedly at her hair with both hands and rearranging the gray silk scarf around her throat. There was, I thought, an air of latent hysteria about her. She had been to see Annette, Giacometti's widow, I knew, and I consequently inquired about the visit.

"She considers you a friend," Isabel said.

"I'm glad to know that," I said. "Annette is not a very trusting person."

"When she first came to Paris, she was only a girl," Isabel said. "She didn't know that trust is like the weather, sun, rain, night and day. Life with Alberto was impossible, and she had to learn everything the way you learn that two plus two equals four unless time bends it."

Bacon said, "Alberto used to say that Annette would never trust anyone she hadn't been to bed with."

"I want more than anything to keep her friendship," Isabel said. "I've known her since she first came to Paris."

Then there was more talk about painting. Bacon remarked—to my surprise—that he didn't care for Goya's "black" pictures but was very impressed by the huge painting of *The Session of the Royal Company of the Philippines*, which he'd made a special trip to see in the museum of the small provincial town of Castres. As great a painting as *The Maids of Honor* by Velázquez, he said. I wonder. He also surprised me by saying how much he admired Vermeer. The mastery of radiance. Not a word about

Rembrandt. More talk about Sonia and Marguerite. I said good-bye after two hours and too much whisky. They were returning to London the following day.

The next meeting with Isabel took place two months later. It was very different from the two preceding it. Having planned to visit London for a few days, I called from Paris to learn whether we might meet without my making the journey to the country. She immediately said yes and suggested that we meet the following Friday, June 12, at the Café Royal at one-thirty. I naturally agreed. She was late, but to my surprise she was clearly sober, seemed composed and genuinely pleased to see me. She declined to have a drink there, suggesting that we might have a bottle of Chablis at the restaurant, whither we could easily walk. It was a well-known place called Wheeler's in Old Compton Street in Soho, a favorite hangout of Francis's, she remarked. She walked at a brisk pace, her hair and scarf blowing back in the breeze, and I thought that if only she could win the battle with the bottle she might recapture some of that irresistible allure which had made men, so to speak, her meat. Her stride was lithe and easy. Something she said, which I couldn't hear because it got wafted off in the breeze, caused her to laugh. That metallic hilarity, like a wild and perilous purring from the Far East. At that moment in the street I could imagine having been swept away by her. However, the past is complete, absolute, a tomb sometimes of overpowering beauty but which we can only visit as helpless tourists. The transience, though, of what is beautiful does not diminish its value. I think Isabel was sufficiently sensitive to realize, and to accept, that we must all make our farewells to rapture and bliss.

Wheeler's was an old-fashioned, well-known, and well-frequented restaurant specializing in seafood. Isabel knew all the staff, probably even the personnel in the kitchen, and all greeted her both as a familiar client and as a notable personality. We sat at a table by the right-hand wall. Our conversation that day was

the most interesting and most moving we ever had. I didn't
learn any facts new or momentous, but what surprised and impressed me was the emotional depth and forceful understanding
that leapt from her evocation of Alberto. She also spoke with
feeling and kindness of Annette, but there could be no doubt
as to which woman had had the more profound and serious
rapport with the man both had loved.

"The thing about Alberto," she said, "that's missed by people
who never knew him and only look at his work but fail to *see*
it, what they miss is the heroic dimension. I'm talking about the
same thing that comes out, you understand, with Beethoven
when you know how to *listen*. I've been very involved with musicians, you see, so I think about it that way."

I said that Alberto also seemed heroic to me, especially since
his death and since I'd started to learn about his life.

"Well, yes, but what you mean, I think, is the legendary aspect," Isabel said. "I mean the heroic dimension in a truly
mythic sense. He lived it out completely to the end. Maybe you
could say that about Rimbaud, too. I'm not so sure. But about
you and me I am. Probably we're lucky to be so ordinary. You
wouldn't say that Prometheus had a very easy time of it, would
you?"

"Hardly," I said.

We drank but a bottle of Chablis, and perhaps I had more of
it than Isabel. I noticed that her hands were relatively clean that
day. She ate fillets of sole with sauce Mornay, one of her favorite
dishes, she said.

There was a little more talk about Alberto, Isabel emphasizing
again that *seeing* was of the essence for him. What he saw, that
is, was far more vital to him than anything he knew. "He had
a problem with the human aspect of things," she said, "and
that's why he considered everything he did to be a failure, because he realized, like Beckett, if you will, that the passion for
representation is doomed to disappointment. And yet the great-

ness lies in the power of the passion. That's what made his work so difficult for him, and what makes it difficult to appreciate at its true value. So it was perfectly natural for him to exist on a sort of razor's edge between despair and ecstasy."

Then we talked about Francis Bacon and his first dealer, Erica Brausen, David Sylvester, and a number of other people, including Marguerite and Sonia, of course. And presently it was time to leave. I had spent a very pleasant moment and hoped that any other meetings I might ever have with Isabel could be just like this one.

It was September before I went again to London. Isabel agreed to meet me for lunch on Friday the thirtieth. She promised to bring with her photocopies of most of the letters she had received from Alberto. We were to meet once again at the Café Royal, and again she was late. This time she did have a drink. She had, in fact, two glasses of champagne. Her conversation wandered, and I suspected that a bit more drink had preceded her arrival. However, she had the photocopied letters in her purse and handed them over—there were only seven—remarking that they probably would tell me nothing that I didn't know already, a prediction that proved to be inaccurate. Even a note that bears a date when set into the mosaic of a lifetime can tell a biographer a lot. We were to have lunch, as before, at Wheeler's, where she had arranged to meet Bacon and several of his friends, one of whom was his new boyfriend, formerly the bouncer in a nightclub the painter frequented. This news did not enthrall me. Bacon alone would have been welcome, but the prospect of added companions, plus bouncer boyfriend, wasn't. Again we walked to Old Compton Street, and Isabel's gait was neither as lively nor as lithe as before.

Bacon and his friends were already settled at a long table by the front window of the restaurant. The others were a radio and television commentator named Dan Farson, and an alcoholic, loquacious writer, plus the new boyfriend, a stalwart, fair-haired

young fellow called Ted, who certainly looked capable of tossing
unwelcome clients into the street. He was seated against the wall
and facing the window, Bacon beside him, Isabel to Bacon's
right and I next to her, Farson opposite Bacon, and the inebriated author opposite me. There were two bottles of champagne
already on the table, both more than half empty. The occasion,
I learned, was to "celebrate" Bacon's having been charged with
possessing drugs, an indictment brought because the police had
found some cannabis secreted in his studio. However, Francis
expected to establish that he had never taken drugs and that the
cannabis had been planted on his premises by a disgruntled former boyfriend, who then foolishly alerted the police to its presence. The artist was nonetheless shaken by the proceedings.
"The police are not polite to pansies," he remarked. "The bas-
tards," Ted added. He could not have been more than twenty-
five or -six but was not in the least shy and seemed quite sensible
in a frankly commonplace manner. Francis was obviously fond
of him, holding his hand affectionately when not busy eating or
drinking. The artist ordered oysters for everyone and more
champagne. Isabel had the same dish as during our previous
luncheon, everyone else some kind of fish. The talk was rambling
and inconsequential. My impression of Bacon on this occasion
was not a pleasant one. He behaved in the strident, devil-may-
care manner so often characteristic of aging homosexuals. It
seemed suddenly to me to bring added poignancy to the question he had asked Alberto: Is it possible for a homosexual to be
a truly great artist? It is, needless to say, possible, but I felt that
Francis's behavior—though, to be sure, he was drunk—somehow gave a negative answer in his case to that unhappy question.
I'd known many artists, two of them incontestably great, and
the great, even the near-great, ones had never given me the
feeling of flabby and egocentric vulnerability that I sensed in
Francis that day. At one moment he remarked, "Nobody knows
how treacherous I can be when so inclined." I wondered about

Bacon's painting. In the light of this remark and his behavior during half the afternoon, the work did not seem to correspond to the man.

The writer suddenly began to vomit. He held his hands up to his face, but the bile boiled between his fingers and splattered on the table, whereupon he leapt from his seat and bolted out the door. "I hate drunkards," said Francis, "and I'll never again say hello to that wretched faggot if I can help it." An observation I thought unbecoming, considering the inclinations of the speaker. The poor man fortunately did not reappear, and the waiters were quick to cover the mess on the table with immaculate napkins. But a fetid stench hung in the air for several minutes, and it seemed to me a sorry token of the entire occasion. After waiting only a few minutes, I said that I must leave. Nobody urged me to remain, though all were perfectly amiable and made a presentable show of warmth when shaking hands as I departed.

Nine months passed, four of which I spent in America, without my giving much thought to Isabel or expecting that it might ever be useful to see her again. After that drunken lunch at Wheeler's, in fact, I had no such desire. Early in June 1971, however, I was invited by a friend to spend a week in London and accepted, thinking I might put some of the time to use by further conversations about Alberto with people there who had known him. I was then still at the stage of taking notes, keeping a detailed journal of my researches and trying to educate myself sufficiently to make a hopeful stab at writing the biography of a man whom I had known but never understood while he was alive. By definition, a biographer is compelled to be devious, because truth is his objective, and it can very easily slip through the fingers of a searcher who is too virtuously fastidious. Even the most conscientious witnesses sometimes must be led by duplicity toward rectitude. Neither is this an easy or pleasant job. At all events, a flagging conscience bid me to telephone Isabel and she laughingly agreed to have lunch with me on Wednesday the ninth. At Wheeler's, needless to say. Even when drunk, which she was on arrival, forty minutes late, she could be very politely English, a picturesque product of the urbane international art and literary milieu, and not an instant of regret or nostalgia dimmed her high-spirited hilarity. She was elated because the drug case against Bacon had been dismissed, the frame-up having been too obvious. But he had had to pay the court costs, a source of much annoyance to the millionaire artist. He was very busy preparing for his large retrospective exhibition in the autumn at the Grand Palais in Paris. My lukewarm interest in Bacon and his art made none of this interesting, and when the conversation pursued its curlicue course around to Alberto, I was not rewarded by much of interest, either. She mentioned the accident to Alberto's foot and said that there had been genuine danger of amputation, which I knew to be false, adding that he'd been many weeks in hospital, also untrue. I asked whether Alberto had ever spoken of marriage when they first knew each other. The question brought forth a great clang of laughter and she said, "Alberto! Why, the mere idea of marriage was like medieval torture to him. The iron maiden. Sometimes he said he'd go back to Stampa as an old man and marry a girl of eighteen. But then he succumbed to Annette's blackmail. Mind you, she's my greatest friend. I'd do anything to help her. And she needs help badly, because she doesn't understand the ways of the world. Strange, isn't it? In a way you might say she's never grown up. And maybe Alberto was too grownup for her. But she will always have my support."

The meanders of talk seeped sluggishly along but unlike their Ionian namesake never got anywhere and also eventually silted up. Even Isabel, I felt, was not dissatisfied when the emptiness of the dining room and the restlessness of the waiters made leave-taking in order. We said goodbye in the street and once again my sentiment suggested that we need never meet again.

Once again, however, it was mistaken. Isabel had been so significant an element of Alberto's life and art that I could not simply eliminate her from my work, or my imagination, and thus her life history grew unforgettably into my own. Her will to live had mastered creative men of exceptional vitality. So why should it not also receive a modest tribute from such a passerby as myself?

A year later, again in June, I was once more in London. To see Isabel had not been my conscious purpose in going there. I had other English acquaintances, all of whom were sociably less challenging. But the very first thing I did upon arriving was to call Sudbury Cottage. It was not so much from a need to see Isabel again for Alberto's sake, so to speak, as from a desire to seek a place of my own in her world. Alan, I knew, had died the previous year, one more husband she had buried. So she would be alone, and that made the prospect of a visit more compelling. I was not afraid, and yet I had a strong sense of some powerful urge drawing me into the outskirts of the jungle where the man-eating creature dwelt. I didn't presume to imagine that I might be worthy prey.

She answered immediately, laughing when I announced my name. She had just returned to the country from London, she said, but suggested that I come down there on Friday to have lunch with her. "It would be a good thing for us to get together," she said, "now that I'm all alone. You can tell me everything that's going on."

"I really don't have anything to tell," I said.

"In that case," she cried, "I'll tell you a few things."

"Anyway," I added, "it will be good to see you again."

"I'll show you some dead birds," she said. "Don't be late. The taxi will be waiting at Audley End."

Mr. Regan was more talkative this time and knew his way straight to the cottage. It was time for lunch when we arrived.

Isabel had obviously been waiting, because the front door flew open before I reached it. She did not come outside, however. The June day was glorious and green, but the air inside the cottage was stale, the light faint. A bottle of Beaujolais already half empty stood on the hearth before a heap of ashes. "Just in time for an apéritif," cried Isabel, pouring out two glasses of wine. Immediately she asked for news of Annette, which I was unable to provide, for by that time Alberto's widow had proved herself more than deserving of the reputation for irascible, vain, and spiteful behavior which, alas, is often the way with artists' widows, and understanding of their predicament does not necessarily beget affection for willful malice. I said nothing like this to Isabel, of course, herself the widow of two composers.

We had lunch, a meal of cold leftovers, in the veranda, where the sunlight was nearly blinding, the view across the fields a verdant, lovely dazzle. More wine was promptly forthcoming. I asked Isabel how she'd learned of Alberto's death. "From the radio," she said, "the first thing in the morning. Annette told me that my flowers were the first to arrive in Stampa. By the way, how fares the biography?"

"I haven't even started writing. It's beginning to look like a very long job. I didn't realize what I was getting into."

"And do you realize how you're going to get out?" Isabel seriously inquired. "I mean *you* as a person. We don't have to worry about Alberto."

"But he's the one I worry about most," I objected. "As a person I matter only as a sort of mechanical apparatus to sort out the facts."

"The facts!" cried Isabel, laughing even more raucously than usual. "The facts will sort *you* out. Beware of the facts, because they aren't the same thing as the truth. Not at all. Not at all."

"Well, I'm not an absolute fool," I rejoined testily. "And don't forget that Alberto cared more for the truth than anyone else we will ever know."

Isabel took a gulp of wine and gazed with her vague eyes

across the ripening fields. After a moment she said, "It killed him, his truth. And it will kill Annette, too. You'll see. Francis, too. You'll see."

"What about Lucian?"

"Not Lucian. He's too ambitious, too tricky, too greedy. The funeral has already taken place."

"You're harsh," I said.

"Not a bit of it," she instantly replied. "Sentimental. I'll grow old. You'll see. And it won't be a picture postcard, believe me. Have a little more wine with your cheese."

We had quite a lot more. She opened another bottle, and then after a while proposed to show me her studio. It was a shed in poor repair in the back yard, a cheerless clutter, dirty and dusty. Several dead birds lay on a listing table. The canvases piled on the ground clearly dated from some time before. She wiped each one with a filthy rag before placing it on an easel for my inspection. Done in drab colors, they were principally still lifes of dead birds, mice, and desiccated vegetables, with an occasional barren landscape in dark earth colors. These were very morbid pictures, touched with an aura of cruelty. I managed to mouth a few hypocritical phrases of appreciation, but Isabel seemed serenely indifferent to comment. I sensed that if I had said that in my opinion her paintings were hideous, she wouldn't have given a damn. What she herself felt about them was impossible to surmise. As we walked back to the cottage through the unkempt garden, I asked her whether she planned to exhibit her work. She shrieked with laughter and said, "Don't you ever dream that you're walking stark naked through Piccadilly Circus?"

There was no answer to that question. When we reached the cottage, Mr. Regan was waiting outside with his taxi. I thanked Isabel for her hospitality, and as I got into the car she said, "Remember to be *very* careful with your facts. When we meet again, there will be time." She laughed and waved, unsteady on her feet, and then the ancient taxi shuddered into motion.

Time for what? I wasn't fearful on the score of facts. Still, it was clear that Isabel meant her admonition as a warning. However, I wasn't convinced of the fidelity of her own relationship with facts. That they could be betrayed by the truth I knew as well as she did. She was elusive, evasive; it was no more difficult to imagine her lurking in a lush Sumatran jungle than striding stark naked through Piccadilly Circus. Unafraid and menacing. Her assumption that we would meet again I considered with caution. And yet she contrived somehow despite the ruin and neglect to make herself majestically commanding. If, after all, after Alberto and Picasso, Epstein, Derain, and Bacon, after the homage of artists and the tribute of nature, she could be bothered with me, then it was my right to respond with fascination. I expected nothing, however. I was relieved to have left Isabel behind in her tumbledown cottage but exalted to feel that she seemed willing to let my life ever so slightly touch her own.

Diego's birthday fell on November 15, a Wednesday in 1972, and in that year it would be his seventieth. Though I knew him averse to anything that concentrated attention upon himself and, indeed, respected his determination to remain, as he always had during Alberto's lifetime, in the obscure background, yet I wanted to make a *fête* of the occasion and felt that he would be pleased if the party could come as a complete surprise. At that time one of his closest friends was Marguerite Maeght, the wife of Alberto's longtime dealer and in her own right one of the most munificent collectors of Diego's furniture. We put our heads together and hatched a scheme. The party would take place at the Maeghts' apartment on the Avenue Foch, but Diego would be lured beforehand to a small restaurant in his neighborhood and from there Madame Maeght would bundle him into her Rolls-Royce. The surprise would be the guests. We drew up a list together, and I insisted that we should try to persuade Isabel to come to Paris for the soirée. We came up with thirty-two names. I called Isabel to invite her. Hesitant and,

I thought, rather aloof at first, she promptly accepted when I suggested that she be my guest from door to door. Her life in the cottage did not suggest that she was materially well off, and it gave me an almost perverse pleasure to be able to pay her way, though I feared she might resent it. She didn't appear to.

We had tea together in the afternoon before the party. Isabel was in high spirits, well dressed and coiffed. Something of the long-ago splendor remained, filling the commonplace salon of the Hôtel des Saints-Pères with remembrance of a Thousand and One Nights. We actually drank tea. She was, as usual, talkative, eager to recall Alberto and Diego in the days of their unknown glory together. Not a word about Annette then. In 1940, she said, she and Alberto often went to eat together at the Brasserie Lipp. Picasso was frequently there as well, and he always stared insistently at Isabel. Principally, she thought, to annoy Alberto, a purpose in which he was expert and invariably successful. One evening he came across to their table and said, "I know how to do her," meaning presumably that he would be better able than Giacometti to execute her portrait. Alberto was incensed. By that time, anyway, his friendship with Picasso had already cooled. After the war, though before Alberto had returned from Switzerland to Paris, Isabel went once with Balthus to the rue des Grands-Augustins and Picasso pulled out three pictures painted in 1940, portraits of Isabel painted from memory, very distorted visages but powerful works of art. He pointedly neglected to offer her her choice but later made a gift of one of them to Michel Leiris, who hung it in the same room with a portrait of her by Bacon, even more distorted than the one by Picasso. "He was not a man any woman in her right mind could care for," she said. We talked for a long time and she told me a number of details about her affair with Alberto, all of which found their way into his biography, so none need be repeated here. She was not at all worried that afternoon about discrepancies between fact and truth, which I optimistically, naïvely, took for a token of trust. I even imagined that I might nearly think of her as a friend.

The party was a grand success. Madame Maeght had asked me to come early to arrange the place cards at the four tables. I put Isabel beside Diego, myself at another table. There were many presents, a cake with seventy candles, and more than enough excellent wine. Diego was embarrassed but delighted. Isabel, alas, was very drunk by the end of the evening and had to be escorted back to her hotel. I didn't see her again during that visit. Though invited, Annette had had sufficient common sense not to come. She and Diego felt only contempt for each other.

The following year, 1973, I was once again in England in June. When I telephoned Isabel, she insisted that I come down to Little Sampford for lunch on the seventh, a Thursday. She was having a party, she said, and I would add to the jollity. I took a magnum of champagne in a large bucket of ice purchased at Harrods, a bit of luggage eyed with unmistakable disapproval by my traveling companions in the train. Mr. Regan was by now positively loquacious and clearly regarded the contents of my bucket with enthusiasm. Isabel, when she saw it, shrieked with pleasure and set aside an almost empty bottle of Bordeaux. Among the other guests was her brother, Warwick, a biologist now living in Australia, who said, drank, and ate almost nothing during the entire afternoon and seemed, I thought, to consider the hilarity of his sister with dour displeasure. Also present was a journalist named Jeffrey Bernard, accompanied by his now di- vorced first wife. He was bright, charming, and a great friend of Francis Bacon, about whom he told a number of very funny but spiteful stories. It was during this luncheon that Isabel related the anecdote of the overturned table at Wheeler's. She had ar- ranged a party there for Alberto during one of his rare visits to London and invited Bacon, who arrived late and drunk after everyone else had begun to dine. He and Alberto promptly launched into a discussion of painting and its difficulties. It started well but then, as Bacon became progressively drunker, developed into one of those maundering monologues about life, death, and the gravity of it all to which Francis was prone when plastered. Alberto, who never drank to excess, listened patiently to all this and eventually responded with a shrug of his shoulders, murmuring, "Who knows?" Taken aback, Francis without a word began to raise the edge of the table higher and higher until all the plates, food, drink, glass, and silverware crashed in a catastrophic clatter to the floor. Alberto, said Isabel, was delighted by such an answer to the riddle of the universe and shouted with glee. The two men did not honestly admire each other's work, but nothing marred the sincerity of their friendship. There was a good deal of talk about sex, and at one point somebody said that perhaps masturbation dulled one's capacity for shared sexual pleasure. Isabel immediately remarked that Alberto would have agreed, "considering his problems." I longed to ask exactly what the problems had been but didn't dare.

The champagne lasted barely to the end of the meal. We had to revert to Bordeaux. "The wine *flows* in this house," Isabel once more succinctly observed. Everyone save Warwick was quite drunk, and I was not sorry when Mr. Regan pounded on the door. But I did regret that there had been no opportunity to renew my sense of acknowledged camaraderie—if that is what it was—with Isabel. This time, however, I felt sure that another chance would be mine.

It didn't come until two years later, a dreary Sunday in February. Isabel had by this time temporarily left Sudbury Cottage, though she still owned it, and was installed in Cambridge. I got her telephone number from Bacon. She explained that she'd moved because the solitude of Little Sampford had begun to get on her nerves and there were numerous congenial people in Cambridge. She asked me to come down and have lunch with her there the following Sunday. I would have accepted in any case, but this time there was almost a tone of pleading in her voice which made it impossible to refuse. She explained with repetitious exactitude precisely how to reach her house and at such length that I felt I could almost have found the place like a homing pigeon.

It was a hideous, small brick house surrounded by huge weeds and nettles, beside an abandoned canal in which the water was covered with green slime. A supremely incongruous element was the presence parked in front of Isabel's house of a large, maroon Rolls-Royce sedan. I had been asked to appear at twelve-thirty, and it was exactly that hour when I knocked on the door. Isabel opened after a perceptible delay. Her hair was awry and wispy, eyes red, cheeks bloated. I had never seen her looking so unwell. She told me that she was busy for the moment and asked me to walk around for half an hour, then come back. I did as asked in that derelict, depressing neighborhood. The iron-colored sky did not promise a clement afternoon. When I came back, the Rolls had disappeared.

Isabel opened the door the moment I knocked and let me inside. I saw only one room of her house, but it was an appalling mess. There were several large tables laden with the remains of heaven only knew how many previous meals and countless empty bottles of Bordeaux, some of them lying on their sides. It was like a scene begging to be painted by Hogarth at his most socially censorious. Isabel invited me to sit down but didn't trouble to ask whether I'd care for an apéritif before pouring some Bordeaux into a glass gray from previous use. She explained that she'd been detained on matters of business with the proprietor of the Rolls and said that her affairs were in a state of nearly inextricable disarray, an estimate I found it all too easy to credit. "But we must go out and have a very good lunch," she said, "to celebrate." She didn't trouble, however, to explain what might call for celebration. Lest it be disaster. Then there was the difficulty we would face in finding a restaurant open on

Sunday. There were good ones, Isabel insisted, very good ones. But they would be shut. It was a bore. "I know all the best ones," she said, "and it's no exaggeration that they know me." She laughed, drained her glass of Bordeaux, and poured herself another. "You're a gourmet," she said, "I'm a gourmet, and the very best restaurants are none too good for us. Too bad we're not in London. Do you know? I sincerely believe that for me Wheeler's would open even on Sunday. For Francis they'd do anything, and if they'd do it for Francis, they'd do it for me. What a pity Francis isn't here right this minute. He'd know how to celebrate." She rambled on and on about the restaurant, Francis, and the necessity for celebration. I sat still, shivering in the damp, chilly house, increasingly ill at ease as I began to wonder whether Isabel was quite the same person I had last seen two years before.

Finally, putting down her glass and shaking herself with what appeared to be grim resolve, she said, "There is nothing to be done. I mean, Francis is a deeply selfish person. I'll just have to fix a little something for us here." Rising unsteadily, she went out of the room, returning very quickly with a tray on which lay a large packet of greasy paper, several ends of cheese and chunks of bread, a plate of butter, and, of course, another bottle of Bordeaux. "Yes," she said, "this will do very nicely." No sooner had the tray been placed on the table than one of Isabel's cats leapt up to inspect it. This feline incursion went unnoticed by my hostess. The paper packet contained several slices of cold ham, which were turning distinctly green around the edges. The cat sniffed at it but turned away with a haughty lack of interest. The butter was streaked with cat's hairs. Isabel did not appear even to glimpse these visual deterrents to an enjoyable repast. She seized two slices of ham, slapped them between chunks of bread lathered with hairy butter, and hungrily munched this cumbrous sandwich, along with gulps of Bordeaux. Loath as I was to do likewise, I didn't want to appear unappreciative and

thought that the odds were against contracting any grave indis-
position. So I followed my hostess's example. The bread was
stale, the ham tasted like copper, and cat's hairs stuck to my
tongue. But the Bordeaux did help. I ate only one sandwich,
no cheese. Then Isabel shouted, "Espresso!" and again left the
room. It was some time before she returned. The coffee was
delicious. As soon as we had finished it, she said, "Let's go for
a walk," and rose unsteadily to her feet. This seemed to me an
extremely bad idea, but I knew better by then than to attempt
to contradict her. Anyway, she was already struggling into a
dirty, ancient mackintosh, and threw open the front door. I put
on my own raincoat and we went out into the misty afternoon.

Walking very close beside her, I kept my right hand ready to
catch her if she fell, which did not seem in the least unlikely.
She weaved precariously as she slowly moved forward but not
once seemed in danger of falling, and I was reassured by the
knowledge that drunken people seldom injure themselves when
falling. She talked incessantly, often repeating after three or four
minutes precisely what she'd said before. It was at best a very
garbled monologue, having to do mainly with Francis and a
dead boyfriend of his named George Dyer, whom, she said,
Francis had consciously willed to die, which Dyer did by his own
hand in Paris shortly before the opening of Francis's retrospective exhibition at the Grand Palais. Then there was a lot of talk
about people I didn't know named Melcher and Deakin and
Bragg and Wirth-Miller and any number of others, talk that
wandered in and out of repetitions, variations, and contradic-
tions to which I paid next to no attention. Never once during
that day was there a mention of Alberto, Annette, or Diego. I
didn't consider the time wasted, because it gave me a somber
glimpse of the destination toward which Isabel was willingly
headed. And yet there was no melancholy attached to the afternoon despite the glowering sky, because Isabel herself appeared
so absolutely determined to pursue the itinerary she had knowingly chosen long, long before.

I was glad to visit Cambridge, admire its quadrangles and especially the magnificent chapel of King's College. Our walk proved to be rather a long one, because Isabel went so slowly, with the result that by the time we came back to her house I had to say goodbye to her at the door in order to hurry to the station. When I held out my hand, she pulled me forward and muttered, "*On s'embrasse.*" So I kissed her on both cheeks, moved by the intimation that she had not been unmindful, after all, of my presence as a person and—who knows?—even as a friend. As I walked away along the rotting canal she shouted, "*Au revoir.* It's only *au revoir.*"

Yet again I was in London in June, but it was four years later, 1979, and by that time I was at last well into the writing of Alberto's biography, an adventure that brought surprises every day. I had not yet reached the advent of Isabel in my hero's life. But I still imagined with complacency that her participation in the adventure had introduced her effectively into my own life.

I arrived on a Wednesday and telephoned Isabel at once. She proposed that we meet for lunch at Wheeler's the very next day, at one o'clock. I arrived in good time, ordered a bottle of Chablis, and waited. I waited and waited. At a quarter to two, famished and having drunk too much, I ordered my lunch. The headwaiter told me he had heard nothing from Mrs. Rawsthorne. Having finished my meal and coffee, I telephoned Isabel. If one may use the word "blandly" to describe her near-hysterical diction, she said that our engagement had been for Friday, not Thursday. The error was mine. I agreed that doubtless it was, though it wasn't. But she hoped that I'd had a good lunch, she said, laughing. Had Francis been there? No. I'd lunched alone. "Well," she said, "tomorrow you shall have my company. One o'clock sharp." And she rang off.

I was there again the next day at one sharp, having reserved the same table, and once more ordered a bottle of Chablis. Expecting to wait a long time, I sipped my first glass very slowly. But this time Isabel surprised me, arriving with what was, for her, almost supernatural punctuality. At only ten minutes past the hour, the front door of the restaurant flew open with a shocking crash and there stood Isabel, disheveled, her hair riotous, one arm flung upward to hold the door open, shrieking with laughter. The clients at nearby tables were visibly startled and appalled, but the personnel regarded Mrs. Rawsthorne with unruffled composure. "I said sharp," she cried, "and sharp it is." She advanced with alarming lurches among the tables as one of the waiters quickly came forward and held out her chair, upon which she fell with an ungainly thump. Clearly she was already very drunk, but I poured her a glass of Chablis all the same. She drank half in a single gulp.

"Are you dying?" she asked. "I'm dying, I must say. Of hunger," she added, laughing her metallic laugh. "Did I tell you I'd been to the doctor? I'm not one for profanity, my dear. Aren't you positively dying?"

The menus already lay on the table, but she knew what she wanted without consulting them. A waiter came promptly and she ordered fillets of sole with sauce Mornay. "My favorite dish," she said. For the sake of simplicity I ordered the same thing. "It's my favorite dish," she repeated, "my favorite dish." She laughed, though I couldn't guess what was funny. Never had I seen her so unkempt and dirty. Her fingernails were so black I thought only surgery could clean them. The conversation was no conversation. She repeated obscure statements as questions two minutes after having uttered them but didn't wait for a reply. "Well," she gasped, "Degas went blind, you know."

Then unfortunately our meal arrived, the fillets of sole in their heavy white sauce. Isabel seized her fork and waved it in the air before plunging it into the fish. The first mouthful went where it was meant to, but the second grazed her cheek, leaving a smear of sauce beneath her eye. She brushed this vigorously away with both hands, transferring the sauce from her cheek to her hair. To my consternation, even as she kept up a largely

unintelligible monologue, punctuated by bursts of inebriated hilarity, her manner of eating did not improve but grew worse.
The plate was only half empty when she threw down her fork
and exclaimed, "Even my favorite dish isn't my favorite dish.
We should have had champagne. *Peu importe,* as Balthus used
to say." But by that time her hands and face and hair were
smeared with thick creamy sauce. The most perfunctory efforts
with her napkin made little difference. She hadn't drunk very
much of the Chablis, however, only three or four glasses. I
longed for her to go to the ladies' room and attempt to clean
herself as best she could, though only a bath by that time would
have sufficed, but she seemed quite unaware that anything about
her appearance might be amiss. The waiters, I supposed, having
doubtless seen her like this before, made no move to help. I
ordered coffee.

"Why haven't you asked about the doctor?" she demanded.

"Oh yes," I said. "I've been meaning to."

"But how could you? They're all such fucking fools. I told
you I'm going to go blind. He said so this morning. I said it's
all in the mind. Who ever heard of glaucoma? That's just something they say to make themselves seem important. Have you
ever heard of it?"

"Not that I can recall," I said.

"I'm not out of my mind," she cried.

"Of course not," I weakly assented, but the films over her
bloodshot eyes suddenly looked grim.

"Rubbish," she said. "But you're not a bit like Francis."

"No."

"Then why don't we go somewhere?" she asked, pushing her
chair violently backward as she wavered to her feet, both hands
on the table to support her.

I paid the bill as quickly as possible, while Isabel made her
precarious way toward the door. Outside on the sidewalk her
appearance, her face and hair still caked with the dried cream

sauce, was even more distressing than in the restaurant. She stood there, swaying back and forth, one hand outstretched as if in search of support, and said, "We must go somewhere and have a brandy. Brandy's the cure. Constant always said so."

It was a dreadful moment. I had an appointment to meet a friend only fifteen minutes later and have always been anxious to be punctual. Yet I hated to leave Isabel in her semi-helpless state there in the harsh daylight on the sidewalk. There seemed no choice, though, and I realized with some shame that I preferred the absence of choice. So I told her that I must go, took her free hand between both of mine, and pressed it hard. "We'll meet again," I said, "soon."

"Soon!" she exclaimed. "Oh yes, the times do change. I take it for granted then. I'm thinking of going back to the cottage. You know, your camellia has done wonderfully well. When *was* that? You call me."

"Yes," I said, turned quickly, and walked away up Old Compton Street. And that was the last time I saw Isabel.

Later that afternoon, when I sat down to record what had happened and been said, my heart felt exceedingly heavy—like the stone which at that moment it undoubtedly was—but there had been nothing I could do, had there? Isabel was possessed by her destiny, and certainly she seemed to confront it without fear. I had only my self-appointed, indiscreet business as an observer. It had been foolish of me to imagine that there could possibly have been anything more.

But I did once again find myself face-to-face with Isabel. A vision of her, that is. The next day I went to the Tate Gallery, where I came upon a portrait of her by Bacon. A wildly distorted image, it nonetheless was an uncanny likeness of the cream-smeared, disheveled, frantic woman I had left on the sidewalk the day before. There was an element of almost intolerable cruelty and sadism in the portrayal of the artist's friend, but he had seen her with terrible acuity, even to the ruin of the eyes, one of them already sightless.

She did return to Sudbury Cottage, leaving behind her works of art in Cambridge at the Fitzwilliam Museum. In the dependable company of her cats and bottles of wine, the years passed her by. As the doctor had predicted, her eyesight failed gradually until she was, in fact, almost blind. And alone. Old friends died or assumed that she must be dead, as they heard nothing from Little Sampford. Circumstances made her a virtual recluse. And then one day late in January 1992 she was found dead. People said it was miraculous she had lasted so long, but Isabel was not one to welcome the end with composure.

The obituaries were numerous and lengthy. All of them, however, dwelt upon the fact that she had been portrayed by many artists, had inspired musicians and done some painting of her own. None even endeavored to elucidate the fact, which was the truth, that all those artists had been impelled to portray her by an ambition to fleetingly capture the wild, fierce freedom of a creature unlike any other. It was an impossible pursuit, needless to say. Isabel alone created her only likeness and in her own time spirited it away.

Part Three

A PALACE IN THE CITY

OF LOVE AND DEATH

———————————————

PEGGY GUGGENHEIM

Exactly twenty times since the first one I have traveled to Venice, and each arrival is invariably yet again the first. Nothing, no memory, no picture—even by Canaletto—can prepare you for renewal of the ecstatic vision that Venice creates and infinitely re-creates. It helps, of course, to be in love when you come to this universally adored abode of human genius, which is slowly, slowly dying. Everywhere in Venice, indeed, the signs of irreversible decay and ultimate decease are visible. It is more and more a city of love—or infatuation—and death. Thomas Mann got it just right. Art, to be sure, is made of love and dedicated to death. And in all the world there is no city more consecrated to art than Venice. So for nearly a millennium travelers have been lured from afar—like the myth-engrossed protagonist of Mann's novella—to submit to the sensuous enchantments of La Serenissima. It was not, perhaps, by accident, therefore, that half a lifetime after Gustave von Aschenbach dreamed himself to death on the Lido another individual preoccupied by the potential of art, and also one far from indifferent to the mythic dimensions of human personality, came to Venice and made a lasting contribution to its magic. This was Peggy Guggenheim.

And when you think about it, Peggy and Venice seem to have been knowingly made for each other. Her story, which is composed almost entirely from themes of art, love, and death, is supremely suited to the city in which she chose to make herself an enduring aspect of its fascination.

In mid-May of 1949, traveling alone on my first trip to Italy, I was in Rome, where I fell in with a couple of other young Americans named Fred Kuh and Ralph Pomeroy, who, like myself, were keen to become familiar not only with Italy's artistic masterpieces but also with its handsome young men. The three of us traveled north via Siena, Florence, and Padua, arriving at last in Venice on June 12. Fred, as it happened, was the nephew of an art critic and curator well known in those days called Katherine Kuh, who had in fact written a review of Peggy Guggenheim's volume of memoirs published several years before, engagingly entitled *Out of This Century*. Therefore, he felt no embarrassment, being in any case a young man difficult to embarrass, about soliciting an invitation for himself and his pals to meet the most eminent American connected with the arts then residing in Venice. Peggy rarely turned away unknown callers who had any pretext, however flimsy, for receiving courtesies which would vary according to the judgment of an extremely discerning eye. She possessed a large, distinguished collection of twentieth-century art, knew its historic and aesthetic value, and was quite prepared to accept the homage owing to her discrimination. We were invited to Peggy's palazzo for a drink. As she had only recently moved in, few pictures were to be seen, most of them being on display in Milan, and the place was not yet entirely renovated, having fallen into some disrepair during the war, when it was occupied successively by German, British, and American troops. It was, moreover, by definition something of a ruin, consisting of only a single story, because the original proprietors had left it unfinished. Nevertheless, it possessed a charm extraordinary for Venice and was ideally suited to an undertaking of personal transcendence which at the time can hardly have been more than a subliminal aura in the new proprietor's concept of her future. Peggy was not a person to stand on ceremony. Talk came easily to us all, helped by drink, and before long our hostess suggested that we dine with her in a nearby trattoria. Before the meal was over, we were on first-name terms. That was my initial meeting with Peggy Guggenheim, easygoing and pleasant, the harbinger of many more in decades to come.

It was by no means, however, my introduction to knowledge of the lively, personable woman who insisted on paying for the dinner of three young fellows who obviously had to be careful with their cash. Shortly after its publication I had read with interest and amusement *Out of This Century*, in which the candor of amorous revelations scandalized her relatives. A good deal more about the author had been learned from various people I ran into in the New York art world, including Jackson Pollock, whose revolutionary career she had literally launched and whom I knew slightly because his wife had had a brief affair with a childhood friend of mine. Peggy's life had not been a happy one. The first calamity came as a consequence of a disaster later viewed as a premonitory prelude to the world-shattering catastrophe so soon to occur: the sinking of the *Titanic* in 1912. Her father was on board and gallantly gave up his place in one of the too few lifeboats to women and children, one of the former his mistress. To a sensitive, sheltered fourteen-year-old girl the sudden accidental loss of a beloved father can cause lifelong trauma. And this is surely what happened to Peggy. She repeatedly stated later that she had never really recovered from her father's death, and her search for compensation led to the amorous liaisons and failed marriages of which the revelation scandalized her relatives fifty years ago but would seem almost innocent today. To enjoy a life considered shocking by puritanical America, it was wise to reside in Europe, especially in France, where the pursuit of erotic satisfaction is more profoundly ingrained and traditional than in any other country. Peggy took up residence in Paris, where she married another American expatriate, had two children, lived the bohemian life, and might have seemed to be embarked upon a permanent career of frivolity and self-indulgence. But love affairs, exciting parties, and frantic travels here and there around the Continent did not satisfy a longing, at first obscure and faint, to participate in something of more enduring and honorable value. As early as 1926, she participated in the opening and operation of a small art gallery in Paris. It was not a success and closed after a single year. But Peggy had had a slight intimation of the power of art to shape human life into a transcendent experience. It took a decade of slowly developing maturity to make a positive reality out of this intimation.

Now, it must be made clear that Peggy was never a woman of great wealth. Her improvident father had sold his share in the fabulously profitable Guggenheim mining consortium well before his death and had so recklessly managed his capital that he would have soon been a ruined man had the *Titanic* not kept its rendezvous with the iceberg. When Peggy came of age, she inherited $450,000. This was no paltry sum in the twenties, but it was not very much by Guggenheim standards, and Peggy always felt like a "poor" relation, which surely had something to do with her attitude toward her relatives and her name. Still, her inheritance was well managed and she was able all her life to do and to buy more or less what she wanted, which is to say that she was a rich woman who had to exercise some caution. This was good for her, and good for art, because it taught her the rules of self-restraint and gave her the determination to seek out only what she believed to be the best.

After a decade of purposeless drifting and affairs with ill-suited, unstable men, one of them the young Samuel Beckett, Peggy finally told herself as she approached the age of forty that it was time to make a decisive commitment in her life toward something that would provide purpose and fulfillment where previously there had been disillusion and caprice. She had frequented the world of artists and writers, felt comfortable in it, and decided to open an art gallery. Not in Paris, where contemporary art was well established, but in London, where it was not. Being a sensible, shrewd woman, she realized that she did not possess as yet sufficient discrimination to select the most important and innovative contemporary works. She needed advice. Her choice to obtain it fell on a man more guilty than any of his numberless followers and imitators of having demeaned the very concept of art as a value which can stand the tests of rational discussion and objective analysis: Marcel Duchamp. He had abandoned painting twenty-five years before and devoted most of his time to playing chess and courting rich women, only occasionally producing some prankish work or object to ridicule the idea of "art." And yet Duchamp was a man of exceptional intelligence and sensibility. He knew what was fine and what was not. The cruel contradiction at the heart of his perceptual being must have been painful in the extreme, but he bore it with panache, and his advice was excellent. He introduced Peggy to Kandinsky, Brancusi, Pevsner, Arp, Tanguy, Cocteau, and a host of others, all of whom she exhibited. She had no notion at this time of forming a collection of her own, but the collection became a reality by *force majeure*, because few works in the exhibitions were sold, and in order to spare the artists a disappointment, Peggy bought from every one of them something for herself. The gallery was named Guggenheim Jeune, partly to honor the famous Parisian premises of Bernheim Jeune, where so much innovative art of the previous century had first been shown, and partly to slyly announce that contemporary art owed something to a member of the Guggenheim clan younger than her Uncle Solomon, whose imposing collection was already widely known.

Guggenheim Jeune became the talk of London, and Peggy

found to her satisfaction that she was something of a celebrity. The gallery was a losing proposition, however, and its proprietor began to contemplate some artistic activity involving less commercial peril. For some time she had been acquainted with a man named Herbert Read, editor of the prestigious art review, *The Burlington Magazine*. He was to become the second astute connoisseur of contemporary art whose counsel she wisely sought and followed. Together they decided to found an institution then regrettably lacking in London but already flourishing in New York, a museum of modern art. Read would resign his editorial post and become director, Peggy assistant director. Consequently, Guggenheim Jeune was to close its doors in fashionable Cork Street and did so with a lively party in June 1939. The moment, needless to say, was not propitious for the founding of a new museum in a city which almost everyone with any common sense realized was doomed to become all too soon the vulnerable capital of a country at war. So the museum project was never pursued beyond the stage of idealistic planning. But Peggy remained undaunted. Her commitment to contemporary art as the pivotal element in her existence had now assumed a life of its own and would ultimately live on after she could no longer serve it.

In the meantime, armed with a list of artists whose works would have been desirable for the nonexistent museum, Peggy departed in August for France, where she drove about the country, meeting and entertaining friends as if no emergency could conceivably be imminent. She was definitely an individual never easy to intimidate. When Hitler and Stalin made their infamous pact, however, soon followed by general mobilization and declarations of war, she realized that a serious situation might soon become perilous and that if she were going to acquire works of art she'd better get busy. Using the money with which she had planned to buy pictures for her museum, she industriously set about acquiring works by the artists on her list, and made it her aim, if possible, to buy at least one painting every day. Within a few months she had acquired more than fifty works of art, often at very favorable prices due to the fear of both artists and dealers that war might devastate not only cities and lives but even the art market. The advice she had solicited was certainly good, but Peggy was the lady with the cash, and much credit must go to her determination and perceptiveness, for among the works she bought during those hectic weeks of daily acquisition were outstanding examples by Brancusi, Braque, Chirico, Max Ernst, Giacometti, Klee, Léger, Magritte, Miró, Mondrian, and others of lesser talent. Meanwhile, the war was coming closer and closer. Ever in character, Peggy worried more about the safety of her art than of herself, arranging to have all of it shipped south before she made any preparations to leave Paris. She realized perfectly well what the Germans would make of the Guggenheim name and only fools were now ignorant of what Nazism meant for Jews. And yet she left the French capital just three days before the enemy marched in, fleeing among hordes of refugees to a small town in the southeast, where she calmly rented a house for the summer. When winter came, though, it grew obvious that she and her two children must get out of France and go home to America. Her collection was very cleverly shipped there before her, labeled as household goods. Peggy went first to Marseilles, where she found a throng of artists and writers, all of them frantic to escape from the fate which they feared the Germans would hasten to inflict. Resourceful and energetic as usual, Peggy did, and paid, much to help these men and women get across the border into Spain, from there to Lisbon, and eventually to America. Among them was the painter Max Ernst, a notorious ladies' man, with whom Peggy fell passionately in love, having long since divorced her first husband, Laurence Vail.

In mid-July of 1941, just thirteen months after fleeing from Paris, Peggy arrived in New York aboard a Pan-American Clipper seaplane, accompanied by Vail, Ernst, a couple of friends, and a flock of children. In order to assure American residence for Ernst, she prevailed upon him to marry her, a grave miscalculation, for her new husband showed her little respect, less love, and virtually no gratitude. But they did live together for a time in a state of continual conflict and confusion, with artists and writers constantly coming and going in a vast apartment overlooking the East River. There were violent scenes and bitter recriminations, followed by brief reconciliations.

Peggy, a woman of unusual vitality and resolve, needed a constructive outlet for her energy. As usual, she turned to art. The plan for a museum to display her collection had remained an active one, and she had kept on buying. The search for a locale in which to exhibit the one hundred and seventy works of art she now owned was presently found on West Fifty-seventh Street, and a highly experimental Viennese architect was engaged to design the museum-gallery, to be called Art of This Century. The outcome was unlike any other that had ever before existed or has been created since, a dreamlike surrealist environment which compelled visitors to look, if they looked at all, in an altered perspective at radically innovative works of art. Paintings were exhibited unframed against curved walls, or floating in space suspended on ropes. The opening in the autumn of 1942 was a sensation, attended even by a few of Peggy's relatives as well as a multitude of avant-garde artists. Enlightened critics perceived that something not only novel but unprecedented had come to New York.

Very shortly after its opening, Peggy and her advisers realized that the museum-gallery should exist not merely as a showplace for her collection but must have a practical commercial purpose as well in order to maintain a vital relationship with the evolving art of that dramatic era. From the first, Peggy determined that her premises should be devoted to the work of young, unknown artists. Her endeavor, she said, would be valid only if it succeeded in serving the future rather than merely recording the past. It was this personal resolve which made Art of This Century a center of creative ferment and assured it a unique position in the artistic history of the very moment when New York was replacing Paris as the foremost center of Western art. The commentators and critics of this period are unanimous in their judgment that Peggy played a paramount role in this evolution. Her gallery was the place where the avant-garde made the rules and anybody was welcome to follow if he could. She enjoyed her work because the conviction of its importance never failed her. At the same time, though, her personal life became a shambles. Max Ernst, whose career and life owed so much to Peggy's inventive determination, abandoned her for a beautiful younger woman, an artist named Dorothea Tanning, whom he married. Peggy was devastated. She was to have other lovers, though no more husbands, but, above all, the primordial importance of her commitment to the art of her century provided an ever consoling raison d'être.

Of all the young, untried artists discovered and aided by Peggy, the most outstanding and, indeed, sensational was Jackson Pollock. The story is that she "discovered" him working as a carpenter in the museum of her uncle, then housed in a familial mansion at the corner of Fifth Avenue and Eighty-eighth Street, although Solomon had already commissioned Frank Lloyd Wright to design and build far larger premises occupying the entire block front facing Central Park. A painting by Pollock was exhibited at Art of This Century for the first time in the spring of 1943, when he was just thirty-one, and it was immediately noticed and praised by discerning critics. Urged by her advisers, Peggy offered the young painter a contract, guaranteeing him a monthly income in exchange for paintings, and gave him a one-man show four months later, when no other dealer in New York would have bothered about him. Success and praise were immediate, and Pollock went on, of course, to become the reigning leader of the so-called New York School and an exemplary figure of the abstract expressionist movement. But even at the height of his fame and fortune he and his wife, Lee Krasner, never forgot how much they owed to Peggy's initial encouragement and support. After Jackson's untimely death in an auto accident, aged only forty-eight, Lee often spoke with emotion of the providential, decisive importance of Art of This Century.

Peggy installed and presented more than fifty exhibitions in her museum-gallery. That this required an enormous investment of work and cash on the part of the proprietor goes without saying. It also goes without saying that no other person in America during this crucial period made so essential a contribution to the developing art of her country. She was unique. This took steely resourcefulness and determination, a starry-eyed belief in the value of what was being done, and even a certain lonely desperation. The highly important artists other than Pollock exhibited by Peggy included Robert Motherwell, Mark Rothko, Clyfford Still, William Baziotes, and many others.

Then one day the war was over. In 1946 Peggy returned to Europe. She found Paris sadly changed. Surrealism was a thing of the past, and after the excitements of the New York art world, the Parisian galleries looked dispiriting and drab. She pushed on to Venice, where she had long dreamed of making a home. But the oneiric city on the lagoon had also suffered from the war— mostly from neglect—and did not yet gleam again with its time-defying loveliness. Peggy went back to New York, but she realized that Art of This Century had done what it could, as had she herself, and others should be allowed to lead the way. Not that anyone ever did so with quite the same verve, generosity, and conviction as she had. The last exhibition took place in May 1947. Peggy ordered the fantastic interior to be entirely demolished—nobody else was to benefit by her originality—and critics wrote that her departure was a serious loss to living American art. Peggy was nearing fifty, and she realized that the time had come to determine once and for all what and where her place in the world of art, history, and the imagination was to be.

The dream of finding a permanent home in Venice had remained an alluring one, and in the springtime of 1948 Peggy rented an apartment in the Palazzo Barbaro, where Henry James had often visited his friends the Daniel Curtises and where he had imaginatively lodged Milly Theale, the hapless heroine of *The Wings of the Dove*. As the Greek pavilion stood empty for the 1948 Biennale exhibition, Peggy was invited to bring her collection from New York and install it there. It created a sensation, for next to no contemporary art had been visible in Italy during the rule of the porcine Duce. At last, in the spring of 1949, Peggy found a residence suitable for the installation and perpetuation of her dream.

The Palazzo Venier dei Leoni is conveniently located on the quiet San Gregorio side of the Grand Canal, halfway between the Accademia and the Dogana. Begun in the mid-eighteenth century, when Venice had long since fallen into irreversible decline, it was meant to be the home of the Venier family, an old and honorable clan, reputed to keep lions on their property, hence the name. If completed as planned, it would have been the largest, most ostentatious palace in the city. But it barely got off the ground, or very much above the water, for the Veniers ran out of money and the project was abandoned after the completion of but a single story. This is an amputated structure of white stone undistinguished save for the ornamentation of eight superbly carved lions' heads just above the water level. It possesses, however, the widest frontage of any palazzo on the Grand Canal and large trees in an exceptionally spacious garden to the rear. With eight windows, an open courtyard, and an ornamental landing stage facing the water, it was saved from monotony by being completely covered in a creeping greenery of wild vines, giving the place a never-never-land aspect of enchantment. For Peggy it was perfect, because she wouldn't have known what to do with fifty or sixty rooms, much less how to maintain them. Eight or ten spacious, airy rooms were plenty, and she was able to acquire the place, as she said, "for a song": slightly more than sixty thousand dollars, in fact an appreciable aria in those days. Peggy's palazzo was unique in Venice, and she had always had a flair for what was unique, turning it ultimately to her own account with hardheaded fixity of purpose.

During that first stay in Venice with Fred and Ralph, I saw Peggy several more times. She was then just about fifty, not a beautiful woman, her hair dyed jet-black, her face marred by a bulbous nose, the result of a botched job performed during the infant era of vanity surgery. But she had a fine, lithe physique. We all knew—from her very own testimony—of her reputation as a female Casanova and assumed that she continued to collect lovers as assiduously as works of art. But she never talked about that aspect of her possessive nature except in terms of the distant past.

Planning to split the cost into thirds, we invited her to lunch at Harry's Bar, an establishment where she was already received with deference. She had long since mastered the art of making herself seem the most noteworthy person at any gathering. This may have been a non-negotiable aspect of the Guggenheim inheritance, although she never made a secret of the fact that she was a "poor" relation. Indeed, one might almost have imagined that she was proud of it. She told us about the troubles she was having with the Italian authorities, who probably considered her a *rich* Guggenheim and insisted upon payment of an exorbitant import duty if the art collection were to remain permanently in the country. It would take a couple of years and entail some movie-style trickery before she could resolve this contretemps.

My second visit to Venice was in May of the following year,

when I traveled throughout Italy with my friend Bernard Minoret, an erudite aesthete whose historical knowledge would fill
a library. Of course we called on Peggy, who had staying with
her a jolly, corpulent Englishwoman called Wyn Henderson, her
onetime secretary and sort of female Leporello during the days
of Guggenheim Jeune before the war. Peggy took a fancy to
Bernard, then slender and dark-haired, with fine features and an
engaging manner. She was seldom shy, especially when a young
man aroused her curiosity. In the habit of sunbathing on the
flat roof of her house when the weather was fine—and that
spring was exceptionally warm—she invited Bernard to put on
a bathing suit, of which she happened to have a surprising quantity of men's models on hand, and join her in the sunshine.
Rarely averse to displaying a physique which had been admired
by Picasso, he was happy to do so. As for me, I have never been
keen to bake in the sun, nor was I invited to. Peggy summarily
suggested that I remain downstairs in the living room with Wyn
and listen to some classical recordings, of which she had an
eclectic collection. That suited me very well. Wyn liked to talk,
cared not two straws for discretion, and told me in detail many
titillating stories about the days of Guggenheim Jeune, the exhibitions and wild parties which took place there, and Peggy's
subsequent adventures in France when she was buying a picture
every day. She also told me a great deal about Peggy's private
life, not much of it very happy or so private as all that, having
been largely described by Peggy herself in print. But Wyn knew
a lot of details that Peggy had omitted, because it had often
been her role to facilitate, as it were, the goings-on of her employer. I wondered, especially as I wrote down the account later,
what Peggy would have thought of the indiscretions of her old
friend. She herself, to be sure, was capable of being highly indiscreet. I also wondered what had happened on the roof above
our heads while we were talking. Not much, as I learned later.
There had been some casual talk of sex, nothing more. Peggy,

I suppose, preferred to be desired by men whose desire for women was unequivocal.

She came to Paris in the autumn of the next year. It was then that she introduced me to her first husband, father of her children, Laurence Vail. His famous charm having washed away on tides of alcohol, he had spent his recent creative impulses decorating empty bottles with driblets of colored wax, splashes of paint, splinters of glass, sequins, and variegated detritus. Peggy courageously praised these creations, proclaiming their value as objects of authentic surrealist vision. She had even devoted an exhibition at Art of This Century entirely to Vail's bottles. I also made the acquaintance of her son, Sindbad, a reserved young man unlikely, I thought, ever to embark upon very adventuresome voyages. Peggy was the only one driven by a strong sense of purpose. That this ultimately had as its aim a craving for self-perpetuation did not diminish either the strength of the drive or the dignity of the means by which she went about attaining its realization.

During dinner she grew nostalgic. The Paris of her youth was lost as Atlantis, she sadly mused. The enthusiasm, the novelty, the excitement were dust-laden memories. Like almost all people of middle age or older—of comfortable means, living in the West, to be sure—she looked back upon "the good old days" as having been fairer, freer, and funnier than the present. Sad to say, her vision was accurate and reflected a reality only too true since the upheaval of the French Revolution. Peggy said that she was glad she would not live to see the year 2000. The world had changed more radically since her birth than in the preceding five millennia. Enough was enough. Everything had changed for her forever when her father died. That event, she felt, was the pivotal one of her life, and perhaps—who could say?—because of it she had been destined to devote herself to the preservation and appreciation of human endeavors that gave to the continuity of life itself in the unpredictable future a meaning and a grace otherwise lacking. That would be more worthwhile, anyway, than an endless cruise on the yacht of Vincent Astor. Peggy was not usually so pensive. It was the only time she ever spoke to me of the death of her father.

Having created for herself without too much trouble a nearly ideal home, Peggy continued to encounter vexing difficulties in making it also ideal for the collection of art which would transform a residence quite modest by Venetian standards into a veritable palazzo. Sovereigns, princes of the Church, robber barons, and latter-day lords of finance have recognized that the possession of great works of art bestows lifetime prestige and the beguiling dream of historical remembrance. How magnificently would Lorenzo loom in our collective memory without Michelangelo? Julius II without Raphael? Frick without Vermeer? Dr. Barnes without Cézanne? Peggy's collection is decidedly not of such venerable company. By generous estimate, it contains no more than a dozen works—by Picasso, Brancusi, Giacometti, and Klee—that might by contemporary criteria be classed as masterpieces, and not one of them has yet had to stand the test of time. But the entire ensemble, no matter what one may think of second- and third-rate artists represented in abundance, is extraordinarily illustrative of creative currents characteristic of their era. Even when choosing a Gleizes or a Marcoussis, for example, Peggy had an unerring eye for what was exceptional rather than merely good. From a certain point of view it was unfortunate that the financial worth of her collection continued year by year to multiply, because the Italians were adamant in their insistence that she pay the import duty, which she stubbornly continued to consider an insult to her commitment as an unselfish patroness of the arts. But if she did not pay she would not be permitted to install the entire collection permanently in her palazzo. In a country notorious for bureaucratic corruption and laxness of law enforcement, such intransigence seems quixotic. Luckily, Peggy was resourceful, and resourcefulness often makes the best of luck. Her collection, still categorized by the Italian authorities as legally in that country only on a temporary basis, had nonetheless been widely exhibited all around Italy in toto or in part. It had become famous, and its fame provided the luck Peggy needed. She was invited to send the collection for exhibitions in Holland, Belgium, and Switzerland. It would, of course, have to be exported, an evaluation at the time of export would be established, and then when the foreign exhibitions were at an end the collection could be imported back into Italy and duty paid according to the value established at the time of export. So it happened that a large truck containing all of Peggy's treasures appeared in the dead of night at a remote alpine border post, where a befuddled customs official irritably let the outlandish cargo pass through at a preposterously minimal evaluation. Thus, when I again had dinner with Peggy in Paris in December 1953, her collection had been happily installed at last in its entirety in the Palazzo Venier dei Leoni, the much reduced import duty having been paid to disgruntled authorities. The foolish men little realized how their obtuse intransigence might have deprived their homeland of a significant patrimony. From that time onward, and for more than a quarter of a century, Peggy, her collection, and her palazzo gradually assumed a single identity which became legendary.

One of the first pieces of sculpture to be permanently installed at the Palazzo Venier dei Leoni was the work of an Italian artist, Marino Marini, and therefore brought no interference from the authorities. Entitled—God knows why—*The Angel of the Citadel*, it was acquired directly from the sculptor in Milan, and represented a horse and a naked rider, the former with its neck and head straining forward, the latter with both arms outstretched as if in ecstasy, head raised toward heaven, and sizable phallus in full erection. This bronze appendage had been cast separately so that it could be unscrewed from the body in case prudish visitors came to call. Peggy was very satisfied with the sculpture, placed it in the forecourt of her house so that it would be visible to anyone passing along the Grand Canal who peered in the direction of her residence. The phallus was seldom hidden from view and caused plenty of gossip in town, where gossip is virtually an industry. Marini was not an artist for whom I had great esteem, but I much admired Peggy's sculpture for its conceptual strength, complex composition, and sensual audacity.

One afternoon in May of 1959, when Peggy and I were alone in the house and I had spoken in praise of the Marini, she said, "Why don't you mount him?"

"What do you mean?" I asked, surprised.

"Ride behind the rider and hold him tight. Wouldn't that explain things? And I'll take a picture from the window here."

The suggestion held a particular appeal, perverse and appropriate at the same time. I did as she asked, climbing up onto the back of the bronze steed and holding the rider tight. Peggy snapped a picture from the living-room window, and perhaps for an imagination attuned to male onsets of sexual excitement the moment offered a provocative appeal. I don't know whether I was the only visitor to the palazzo invited to ride the Marini. Probably not. Sindbad Vail, prompted by a cultural aspiration of his own, had gone into the business—risky at best—of publishing a little magazine devoted to literature and the arts called *Points*. In the spring of 1950 he published a short story by me entitled *The Lizard*. It is the tale of a young man's approach to maturity and contains a detailed description of masturbation. Peggy was very much taken with this passage, said it was the best evocation of an orgasm she had ever read, and insisted that I copy it word for word into her guest book, which I did with reluctance. I later wondered whether she put the snapshot of me on the Marini into her book along with the fictional orgasm.

It was during the Venetian sojourn of 1958 that Bernard and I were joined there by Dora Maar. We took her to meet Peggy, as it seemed fitting that two ladies who had in one way or another made themselves important to the art of their era should come face-to-face. Peggy was always content to parade her pictures and I thought she'd be flattered to have under her roof a woman who had so often inspired Picasso. The meeting was not a success, because both ladies liked being catered to, though not at all in the same manner. When we left the Palazzo Venier dei Leoni, Dora said, "Madame Guggenheim merits our compassion, but she wouldn't know how to go about being worthy of it." Bernard asked what that meant, and Dora replied, "That's the mystery."

In those gilded, foolproof years, when the tourist tidal wave was but a ripple and no garbage yet littered the Piazza San Marco, Peggy owned a gleaming speedboat. It was driven by a mechanic as handsome as the craft. We used to course across the lagoon to deserted beaches where the water was clear as glass and swim up and down the sandy strand where later we ate chicken sandwiches and deviled eggs and drank icy Torgiano Bianco. Peggy never seemed more content. The palazzo was open to the public three afternoons a week during the season, entrance free, and if visitors did not arrive en masse, those who came seemed genuinely interested in what there was to see.

Peggy did not spend all her time in Venice, a city less miraculous to the eye when drenched in freezing rain, though breathtaking beneath the rare, pristine snowfall. She traveled back and forth across the world, visiting friends and acquaintances, museums, the ruins of lost civilizations. Receptions were given in honor of the lady people remembered, or had heard of, as the queen of the Venetian avant-garde, if such a group could reasonably be thought to exist in a city doomed to cultural and political decline for more than three centuries. If Peggy had become a celebrity, the city of her dreams had very appreciably contributed to her fame. As the years added up to decades, however, she cannot have failed to recognize that the twentieth century was proving to be the most perilous of all for Venice. While

Henry McIlhenny in 1981, seated in his drawing room beneath the Degas *Interior* (*left*)

[Photographer unknown]

Glenveagh Castle seen from mountainside to its rear (*below left*)

[Gloria Etting]

1914 Rittenhouse Square, with house to left in which Henry installed his ballroom (*below right*)

[Photographer unknown]

Isabel Rawsthorne about 1937

[Photographer unknown]

Bust of Isabel by Jacob Epstein, 1933

[Photographer unknown]

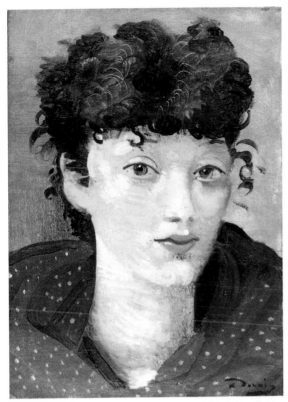

Isabel by André Derain, 1935
[Photograph used with kind permission
of Fitzwilliam Museum, Cambridge]

Isabel by Alberto Giacometti,
1937
[Photographer unknown]

Isabel by Picasso, 1940

[Christian Zervos]

Isabel by Francis Bacon, 1966

Sonia Brownell in *Horizon* office in 1949, with Lys Lubbock in background
[Used with permission of Orwell Archive, University College, London]

Peter Watson in 1947
[Cecil Beaton]

Palazzo Venier dei Leoni in late fifties. Note speedboat at lower right

[Photograph courtesy of Karole Vail]

Author in 1959 astride Marino Marini
sculpture in courtyard of palazzo

[Peggy Guggenheim]

Gondola days, author and Peggy
in 1975 (*left*)

[Photographer unknown]

Legendary Peggy enthroned in
the garden of her palace in 1975
(*below*)

[Camera Press, London]

Ethel Bliss in her youth

[Photographer unknown]

Ethel Platt in old age

[Photographer unknown]

Rear façade of Ethel's house, with large window in center from which she gazed
out toward her meadow

[Page Kidder]

the tourist tide rose higher and higher, encouraged out of unscrupulous financial greed by municipal authorities, the waters
of the lagoon did likewise, periodically flooding the city's
squares, alleys, and the lower floors of palazzi, doing damage
which the authorities struggled in vain to prevent. Worldwide
appeals to "Save Venice" were mounted. Much money was contributed. Where it went nobody knew. Tourists and floods continued to increase in quantity and noxiousness. Throngs of
young visitors from the north and east arrived with packs on
their backs to spend a single day but not a single lira, eating
enormous sandwiches on the steps of the Piazza and leaving
behind heaps of refuse, not to mention graffiti scratched into
the tender marble of churches and palaces. Even the cellar of
Peggy's palazzo was flooded, and dripping "drip" paintings by
Pollock had to be rescued in extremis. Worse than the flooding
was the air pollution caused by fumes from the chemical factories
of the unscrupulous Count Volpi, Mussolini's crony, located but
three miles away in Mestre. Delicate statuary on the façades of
churches appeared afflicted by leprosy and the famous Greek
horses of San Marco had to be replaced by copies. And yet the
authorities did all they could to attract more and more and more
visitors even as the local population steadily moved away to the
mainland. The winter carnival was revived, cut-rate tours out of
season were advertised, the film festival pursued its frivolous
folderol, and the semiannual art exhibition, the world-famous
Biennale, its prestige a joke, exhibited crushed automobiles,
heaps of boulders, neon signs, and odd lots of hiking boots.
Peggy cannot have been blind to the precipitous downward spi-
ral, but she had committed herself, her collection, and, thus, the
cumulative significance of her raison d'être to Venice. There
could be no turning back.

It seems never to have occurred to her that this absolute and
prodigal commitment to Venice might cost her anything. She
had at her own expense built an additional exhibition gallery in

the garden, providing space at last for every interesting work in the collection, plus a few that testified to fallible judgment as she grew older. That the gift of palazzo and contents represented a munificent benefaction nobody could have doubted. Other questions, however, less lustrous, needed to be answered. The first was the thorniest. Was the city of Venice ready, able, or, indeed, eager to assume responsibility for the upkeep and conservation in perpetuity of the Palazzo Venier dei Leoni and the Peggy Guggenheim Collection? The answer was no. Venice was already overcrowded with masterpieces of architecture and art that it could not afford to maintain or protect from the threat of subsiding into the sea.

Now it was that the impetuous decision of Benjamin Guggenheim to part from the mining business of his brothers came most unhappily home to roost. If Peggy had been as rich as her cousins, the future of her palazzo and her collection would have been assured, because she would have been able to leave an endowment sufficient to maintain them. But she had only enough to live on, and her monetary legacy would be next to nil. All she had was very rich relatives, of whom only one, her Uncle Solomon, had shared her passionate interest in art and a determination to leave behind an institution bearing his name.

By 1971 the speedboat was but a memory. Visiting Venice in September of that year, I found Peggy changed. She was no longer so gaily lighthearted and openly proud of her possessions as before; some *élan vital* seemed to have been lost. She had to face the inevitable fate awaiting her collection. If she wished it to remain forever in her palazzo in Venice, some institution with sufficient funds had to make a binding commitment for its upkeep. Only one institution in the world was prepared to do so: Uncle Solomon's Foundation. Its administration was still very largely a family affair, and to Peggy, aged seventy-three, familial considerations meant more than they did in the era of her prewar self-indulgence. She had agreed to exhibit her collection in the Guggenheim Museum in New York in 1969 and a year later consented to deed all her property to the S. R. Guggenheim Foundation with the proviso that the works of art should be exhibited ad infinitum in the Palazzo Venier dei Leoni, or somewhere on the nearby mainland if the city should finally sink. The institution thus created was to be called the Peggy Guggenheim Collection. Harry Guggenheim, Solomon's nephew and president of his foundation, once a critic of her carryings-on, wrote, "Come home . . . All is forgiven." And so the future was taken care of. Once again luck had been generous with Peggy, and it is only fair to say that her passion for art had made her eminently deserving.

In 1973 she had another stroke of luck. Visitors to the collection were becoming more and more numerous. She needed someone both knowledgeable and dependable who could live in the house, receive visitors, sell catalogues, and act both as a curator and as a guest to keep her company. Such a person was by no means easy to find, as Peggy upon occasion could be difficult and capricious, and was not well known to be openhanded. The man she found was someone with whom she had been acquainted for years. His name: John Hohnsbeen. John had by this time been a well-known citizen of the international art world for close to twenty-five years, having drifted here and there on the currents of gallery employment and sentimental opportunity. Good-looking and a good talker, well mannered and tolerant, though not addicted to hard work, he was as nearly an ideal companion for Peggy as she could have prayed for. Living in Rome when her proposal materialized, he moved to 701 San Gregorio as if Clotho herself had prepared for it. Except for the winter months, when the palace was closed and its inhabitant traveled to more clement climes, John kept by Peggy's side as long as she lived.

The speedboat was replaced by a gondola, the handsome mechanic by a rather grizzled gondolier. It was the last private gondola in Venice, and Peggy was the last picturesque, eccentric, provocative character to ride in one. She loved the funereal craft and her daily late-afternoon driftings through the spellbinding, decrepit old city, always directing the gondolier herself. She knew almost all the hundred and fifty canals, the names of at least two-thirds of the four hundred bridges, remembered who had lived where and related with relish the dramas that had taken place in crumbling palazzi. It was a rare pleasure to go along with her, gliding silently upon the black water. Malicious Venetian tongues maintained that she took to the gondola because she'd grown too lazy to walk. The truth is that walking had become difficult for her. In the old days she had worn one out with her brisk pace through the city. No longer. Now she was anxious to find companions for rides in her gondola, and this was not always easy. She had her dogs, of course, had always had them, fluffy little Lhasa terriers she called her babies and loved, perhaps, more than people. But they could not converse with her and she liked to be listened to. I was always happy to keep her company, as I sensed a basic loneliness and melancholy beneath the public persona, the famous connoisseur and collector and so-called Ultima Dogaressa. One afternoon in the autumn of 1975 as we were drifting along a quiet *rio*, when conversation had temporarily lapsed, it occurred to me for some reason I didn't understand to ask her a personal question. "Tell me, Peggy," I said, "who are your really close friends?"

She didn't seem a bit surprised, but Peggy was so self-contained that it was difficult to imagine her showing surprise at anything. Having considered the question for a minute or two, she said, "Well, you're one of them." I was astounded. Nothing had ever given me cause to imagine that she felt so. And yet I was not displeased that she might think of me as a close friend, and I transposed my pleasure into a conviction that I had always appreciated in Peggy a directness and easygoing spontaneity which could pass for genuine warmth without, I surmised, either truly offering anything to others or quite asking them for anything in return. This made relations with her simple, though I wondered whether she could find them truly satisfying. No matter. It was she, after all, being a lady and appreciably older, who determined their character.

In any case, not long after returning to Paris I had occasion to write her a letter, conveying information about a specialist in circulatory troubles which she had asked me to obtain. I took advantage of that opportunity to tell her how deeply touched I had been by her feelings for me as a friend and how for my own part I had long felt sincere affection and admiration for her not only as a person but also, so to speak, as an institution. Needless to say, I had never before written to her in such a vein, and some hyperbole worked its way into my letter, but it didn't seem inappropriate after what she had said to me in the gondola. In due time she answered as follows:

Peggy Guggenheim Foundation
6 October 1975

Dear Jim,

Thank you so much for your most amusing letter. At first I took it seriously and could not believe it. Then I realized it was a joke and loved it.

Thank you for the name of the doctor. I am not coming right away. I have been given another two months' respite. So we'll be coming along later. I'm also to have a show in Turin in the modern museum in early November, so I don't know how things will fit in.

In the meantime I have promised to write a book of memoirs with the French Consul General here. He has found a publisher who offers me a fifteen thousand dollar advance and, I think, sixty percent of all foreign rights and film and theater, etc. His name is Albin Michel. He wanted me to sign the contract and came to Venice on purpose but I refused until I had an agent. Can you produce one? The French consul is going to ask me questions and take it down on a tape. I have promised him one-third. He seems to be the general inspirer. I think he expects to make a lot out of it but says he is not interested in the money. Anyhow, please produce a good agent.

The gondola days are over, sad to say. It's getting pretty autumnal.

Gypsy has terrible asthma. I took her to a vet in Udine. Five hours in the train and three in the doctor's waiting room. Into the bargain I lost a key of a cupboard there. The cupboard contains everything, including catalogues and books and wine and toilet paper, so I am going mad over the weekend till I can get a locksmith. Thirty keys in the house and not one would open it.

Love,

Peggy

I was surprised and saddened to be told that Peggy had believed my letter to be a joke. Only a person, I felt, resolved not to take seriously the potential seriousness of human relationships could have imagined it to be facetious. As I thought about it, I could not keep from concluding that the incident revealed something basic in Peggy's nature, and the more I thought about it, considering all I knew by this time about Peggy, her life, her relations with other people, her career as an art collector and dealer, the more basic and melancholy I felt the revelation to be.

The plan for the book of memoirs came to nothing. Instead, Peggy herself composed a revised and amended version of her own two previous books of memoirs, *Out of This Century* and *Confessions of an Art Addict*, the latter first published in 1960. For this final publication she reverted to her first title and the revised edition of *Out of This Century* appeared in 1979 very shortly before her death. She probably had the pleasure of holding a finished volume in her hands but fortunately did not see the hostile review which appeared in *The New York Times* on the very day she died. The next morning the same newspaper published the news of her death on its front page, followed by a long and detailed obituary.

In May of 1977, I had yet again visited Venice. Peggy complained on the telephone of feeling unwell and walked with difficulty but agreed that we should dine together in a small restaurant very near her house. During dinner we talked almost exclusively about her health, her affairs, and her worries. Her view of the future was, to say the least, somber. She complained about John, saying that he cared nothing for the collection, which I knew to be untrue, and was interested only in gossip and cocktail parties, which was not altogether false, an interest, to be sure, which Peggy herself had blithely shared in more felicitous days. She would not be around much longer, she said, and would not be sorry to go, having, after all, seen everything, known everyone, and been everywhere. It was a decidedly gloomy evening.

We walked back together, Peggy almost limping, to her garden gate, an affair of open ironwork embedded with rough lumps of colored glass, the work of an American named Claire Falkenstein. Arriving there, Peggy discovered to her annoyance that she had forgotten her key. It was late. The garden and the house beyond were dark. Peggy was obliged to ring the bell, to ring it, moreover, repeatedly, until finally a sleepy man's voice came through the intercom, accompanied by considerable static, demanding to know who was outside. *"Sono io, la signora,"* Peggy replied. The man at the other end evidently did not understand, for he again asked to know who was there and Peggy gave the same answer. Still he did not understand, obliging Peggy again to repeat herself. The intercom must have been in poor repair, because this went on for several minutes, until Peggy was fairly shrieking again and again with comprehensible exasperation, *"Sono io, la signora,"* finally adding rather plaintively, *"La signora . . .* Guggenheim!" And it seemed, indeed, a conclusive mortification that in order to be admitted to her home, albeit late at night, she should have been compelled to make herself known to her own servant by the name which for half a century had served her endeavor to make herself known to all the world. There was silence then from the intercom, presently lights went on in the garden, a man appeared, looked out through the gate, and, seeing Peggy, burst into profuse apologies as he opened it before her. She was visibly not going to be easy to placate. I told her good night, said I would call in a day or two, kissed her on both cheeks, and walked back toward the Accademia.

She had become obsessed by death as she approached the age of eighty but was still able to enjoy a gala celebration of that birthday at the Gritti Palace Hotel. Little more than a year later she lost her balance when descending from her beloved gondola, fell, and broke her hip, the injury most feared by the elderly. Hurried to the hospital in Padua, she underwent the inevitable operation. It failed. Having suffered a stroke, she fell into a coma and died two days before Christmas in 1979. So, alas, she was denied the consecration of death in the city she had very probably loved more sincerely than she had any human being. Her ashes, at least, were interred in the palace garden alongside the graves of her babies.

Peggy dedicated her life to the proposition that art is the noblest and most valuable of human creations. She did so not only by gathering a unique collection of art of this century but also by helping many of its most significant practitioners to make their way in a difficult, often indifferent, world. By doing this she managed, as she suspected she might, to outlive herself in the city where love and death have supremely made the most of mankind's transcendent dream. Her palace, now bearing her name on its façade, testifies to the daring, imagination, and dedication of a woman who surpassed herself by becoming the personification of an ideal.

Part Four

BEYOND *HORIZON*

———————————

SONIA ORWELL

AND PETER WATSON

With Sonia I was lucky. I met her first when she was still happy, beautiful, and charming. Before Orwell died. Before Peter died or, as I believe, was murdered. Before Cyril fell into irreversible decline. Before her mad marriage to the homosexual millionaire not long out of prison. Before she gave cause to be described in a book entitled *Difficult Women*. All that was long ago, and now she's dead. But how charming, how beautiful, how happy she truly was in that cozy, homely flat at 18 Percy Street. Her laughter was like a flight of larks during those intoxicating years when the war was not yet a distant memory.

On October 11, 1949, I traveled from Paris to London with Stephen Spender, Bill Goyen, and Robin King. We took the train, the boat from Calais to Dover, another train to Victoria Station. Stephen needs no introduction. Bill, an American writer of modest but honorable distinction, was Stephen's lover of the moment. Robin, a British critic I'd met in a bar in Paris and of whom nothing has now been heard for decades. But at the time he knew everyone in the British literary world and had presented me to Graham Greene and Angus Wilson and his aggressively working-class boyfriend Anthony, among others. Stephen I'd met in New York the year before. It was Robin who had sent one of my short stories to Sonia. She liked it and showed it to Cyril Connolly, editor of *Horizon*, the most prestigious literary review of that faraway era, and he accepted it for publication in what turned out to be the final issue. That was why I was going to London, where the day after my arrival I met Connolly in *Horizon*'s office at 53 Bedford Square. He was friendly and flattering, introduced me to the two other persons present, Sonia Brownell and Peter Watson, and invited me to a party at his flat the following evening. It was my first introduction, a superficial one, to the literary, artistic, and social world in which I longed to find—and to deserve!—a rightful place.

It was Robin, of course, an inveterate gossip, who told me everything he knew about Sonia, Peter, and Cyril, and he knew nearly all that anyone knew. Sonia had been born toward the end of World War I in India, daughter of an Englishman in business there who died while she was still a child. The widowed mother eventually brought her children back to Britain and ran a boardinghouse in London. Her rigid bigotry led her to confine Sonia during her entire adolescence to an ultra-strict Catholic convent, with the predictable result that the grown woman nourished a ferocious loathing of prudish bias and a crippling mistrust of emotional entanglement. Among her friends she was regarded with humor as an impenitent spirit for her habit of spitting whenever she glimpsed a nun. Robin believed that it was her misfortune rather than good luck to be exceptionally beautiful, with rich golden hair, brilliant eyes, a fine oval face, and voluptuous physique. Men were inevitably attracted to her and she had a few affairs but grew skittish when attentions became pressing. She had intellectual ambitions. Her intellect, however, had not been fortified by the insipid curriculum of the convent. In order to compensate for that shortcoming, she endeavored to cultivate men of literary attainment and, if possible, famed for creative brilliance. She proved adept at this, and there were those who joked that her stockings were too blue to be true. Having become acquainted with Connolly, she managed by dint of pertinacious hard work—in the beginning without pay—to become an important member of *Horizon*'s small staff, thus gaining entrée to the wide but rarefied circles of the literary and artistic world in London. The most imposing measure of her success was a proposal of marriage from George Orwell, the celebrated but ailing author of *Animal Farm*, whose recently published novel, *Nineteen Eighty-four*, in which Sonia is an easily recognizable character, was even then a sensational success both in England and America, selling over four hundred thousand copies in one year. Despite her aversion to emotional entanglement, Sonia had found Orwell's proposal difficult to refuse, *Horizon*'s days being now definitely numbered and her resources limited. Some maliciously murmured that she took seriously the novelist's suit for pecuniary reasons, but as things turned out, her marriage to Orwell did not make Sonia rich, or even comfortable till years later. It lasted only three months and eight days. Then there were very high death duties to be paid, and a considerable portion of the inheritance went to an adopted son. At all events, it seems that Sonia in her brash way was sincerely devoted to the famous author, though she clearly did not return his earnest love. As a man he cannot have appeared to present a very virile threat to her ambivalence, because his health was precarious. During the Spanish Civil War, fighting against the Fascist forces, he had been badly injured, his lungs as a consequence condemning him to a condition of gradually deteriorating convalescence. The marriage, in fact, took place in a hospital room, which he was never to leave, the ceremony performed the very next morning after my introduction to the bride. The new Mrs. Orwell appeared that same afternoon, radiant, at a celebratory cocktail party given by Cyril Connolly in his spacious flat at 25 Sussex Place.

I was decidedly overawed. Everyone present seemed to know

everyone else, and I assumed that the other guests were eminent and accomplished, while I not only knew nobody but was nobody. So I tried to make myself inconspicuous and admired the works of art. A fine, fragile Giacometti, *The City Square*, was set out on a table behind a couch, and a beautiful, haunting painting of a girl on a ladder set against a cherry tree hung on a side wall, the work of a painter then nearly unknown named Balthus. There were other pictures by artists I'd never heard of. The aura was one of elite and luxurious refinement. Cyril Connolly was a gracious but somewhat remote host. An ugly, jowly, pug-nosed, overweight man, he possessed rare charm, speaking with eloquence as if he knew every last thing there was to know about civilization and generously consenting to pronounce clairvoyant judgments when pressed. Of course I had read many issues of *Horizon* and his brilliant introductory "Comments" as well as *The Unquiet Grave* and *The Condemned Playground*, his volumes of criticism, bookish erudition, and autobiographical meditation, so I knew that he publicly condemned himself as a slothful failure, a man who made his glory of self-mortification and knew in his jaded heart nonetheless that posterity would let a modicum of laurel settle on his inanimate brow. All this made him to me rather intimidating. We did not become friends and I never again set foot in Sussex Place. I saw him several times at Bedford Square. And he did publish my story, "The Boy Who Wrote NO," in *Horizon*. He said of it in the "Comment" introducing that final issue: "The short story is one of the first works to be printed by a young American writer and continues the line of honorable craftsmen with strong feelings like Truman Capote, Paul Bowles, Eudora Welty, Paul Goodman and Donald Windham whom we have helped to disseminate in this country and their own." Though I was more than content with such praise, it was only the intoxicating proximity to Miss Welty that gave me hope of reputable achievement someday. Even then, I had no high opinion of the others, nor has it risen since. Cyril proved that my story, the only acceptable bit of fiction I have ever written, had truly earned his esteem by republishing it three years later in *The Golden Horizon*, an anthology of the works he judged the best that had first appeared under his editorship. I ran into him occasionally in Paris, but he was always holding forth to other people and I was never invited to be one of them. Years later I heard a lot about Cyril from Barbara Skelton, the second of his three wives, a woman incapable of friendship, with whom I thought myself friendly. In her two volumes of superficial, mendacious memoirs she has a lot of derogatory things to say about Cyril, all of which make him seem to have been appealingly unhappy.

During the two weeks I spent in London, a chandelier created by Alberto Giacometti arrived in the office at Bedford Square. It was an intricate, airy, imposing bronze work. Peter Watson and the sculptor were friends. I felt privileged to have a hand in helping to suspend the splendid fixture from the ceiling while the electrician did his job with the wires. Peter I found just as appealing as I found Sonia, perhaps more so, since he was a man who shared my fondness for men. He was attractive, too, because of a certain melancholy reticence. One felt that the gentlest tap of a magic wand would transform him into a beautiful prince attired in cloth of gold and wearing a royal crown, the hero of a tale by Hans Christian Andersen. And, indeed, for me he did turn out to be magical, because it was thanks to him that my life and my view of the world were entirely transformed. But this did not occur until a couple of years later.

Peter was the only true patron of the arts that I have ever encountered. Compared to him, Charles and Marie-Laure de Noailles, for example, were mere seekers after novelty and diversion as an alternative to the conventional constraints of a staid and effete aristocracy. Peter was not an aristocrat, although in the truest sense of that term he embodied the exalted ethos of a bygone era. His father had been a nouveau riche whose enormous fortune flowed from the manufacture of margarine, not considered a noble source of wealth. When he died, Peter was only twenty-two, and from that time until the end of his life he had a very great deal of money. After a period of youthful extravagance and self-indulgence, which included the acquisition of many fine works of contemporary art, he spent his fortune with such superlative finesse and lack of ostentation that one who knew him slightly might have thought him a person of moderate means. His luxurious youth was spent mostly in Paris, where in the rue du Bac he shared an art-filled flat with an American boyfriend of exceptional beauty but very volatile temper named Denham Fouts. Peter contemplated founding a review which would illustrate the foremost trends of contemporary painting and sculpture. But 1939 put an end to that plan. Fouts returned to America, Peter to London. Rejected for military service because of fragile health, he didn't know quite what to do with himself. Cyril Connolly, who had been acquainted with Watson for several years, had a ready and pressing proposition. Together they would found a monthly review dedicated to literature and the arts, having Cyril and Stephen Spender as co-editors, Peter as financial sponsor. With England at war and the future for everyone and everything highly uncertain, the moment can hardly have appeared promising for the debut of a publication dedicated to the perpetuation of values which warfare dooms to irrelevance. The would-be publishers, however, were quixotic young men who believed that the grand purpose of warfare should be to perpetuate the very values most threatened by it. And so *Horizon* began its career amid doubt and peril, the first issue appearing in mid-December 1939. To the surprise and delight of everyone concerned, it was an instantaneous success, received prestigious commendation in the press, and required two reprintings to satisfy the demand. Spender soon relinquished his post as co-editor, leaving Cyril and Peter in entire control, the latter, as was his wont, keeping diffidently in the background, save where art was concerned, but supplying the necessary cash, while Cyril, as was *his* wont, serenely took credit, though with many a moan over the labor required, for maintaining the brilliant success and intellectual distinction of the magazine. It must be acknowledged that he deserved the credit, for his uncompromising discrimination assured both the distinction and the success. And so things continued throughout the war and for five years after its end. A decade is a relatively long life span for a small literary magazine, and by the end of that time Cyril had begun to weary of continuing responsibility and to fall into periods of negligent self-pity, while Peter had grown tired of his editor's morose sloth and cavalier way with expense accounts. Thus, the magazine by common consent announced its forthcoming demise. It was just at this juncture that I first appeared in Bedford Square, met Cyril, Sonia, and Peter, and got invited to Cyril's party. Peter had also planned a party to celebrate Sonia's illustrious marriage and he invited me to attend.

In the small apartment at 10 Palace Gate I felt far more at ease than in Cyril's more imposing residence. One might almost have thought that Connolly was the rich man, Watson the one compelled to pinch pennies. Except that Palace Gate had more and finer works of art than Sussex Place. There were things by Braque and Chirico, Juan Gris, Giacometti, Rodin, Henry Moore, and others, all obviously chosen by a connoisseur's severely discerning eye. Moreover, Peter was warmly friendly, made a point of introducing me to a number of the others present, among them two painters who happened to be my exact contemporaries: John Craxton and Lucian Freud. The former became a lifelong friend, the latter a very temporary one. But both of them later drew portraits of me. John was, and remains to this day, one of the most happy-go-lucky, unassuming, and least arrogant persons anybody could hope to meet. Lucian became just the reverse. They had been close friends in early youth,

working in adjoining studios paid for by Peter. But the friendship did not survive Lucian's ravenous *arrivisme*. John went to
live in Crete, where he painted some handsome pictures and
made no effort to gain celebrity. Lucian remained in London,
worked wonderfully well for a time, then grew vain, irascible,
and snobbish, achieving wide fame with poor paintings and, after Francis Bacon vacated it by dying, the dubious niche of
Greatest Living Artist.

Among Peter's friends it was regarded as a rare distinction to
have a story published in *Horizon*, especially in the final issue,
and consequently something of a fuss was made over the unknown author, who was both thrilled and troubled by attentions
not necessarily durable. Peter invited me to lunch, during which
I was intimidated by his princely manners. John invited me to
tea in the vast, somewhat ramshackle house in Hampstead in-
habited by his numerous family, all of whom seemed to be musicians. Some of them are still there, still musical, because the
last time I was in London I went out to Kidderpore Avenue for
lunch, John being briefly at home on one of his rare visits from
Khaniá. But it was Sonia more than any of the others who at
the time seemed to take to me the most.

I didn't wonder why, imagining myself settled despite misgivings on the merry-go-round of literary doings and being too
foolish to discern the fickle, precarious operation of the carnival. I, of course, liked Sonia, too, and then I was new, excitably
responsive to any sign of approval. And I was American. In 1949
a bittersweet remnant of appreciative sentiment still clung to the
idea that the New World had come to the rescue of the Old in
its time of peril. Moreover, like Peter, to whom Sonia was ef-
fusively devoted, I was homosexual, therefore presenting no
danger of involvement. She had cleverly learned from Cyril the
arcane tricks of the editorial trade and brought with her one day
to tea at Percy Street the manuscript of my story, pointing out
several ways in which it could be improved, all of which I was

sensible enough to accept. It was not the last time that she lent an experienced helping hand to my writing and to my would-be career.

She had also invited that afternoon another aspiring American writer, Waldemar Hansen, whose love affair with Peter was just then hobbling to its mournful conclusion. Hansen was dejected and resentful, having been an honest and serious lover and admirer of the older man, whose support had temporarily transformed his life. He had been too nice to Peter, Sonia maintained, altogether unlike Denham Fouts, who had been impossible, addicted to drugs, furious rages, and odious insults. But Peter had been obsessed by him. Oh, he was beautiful, yes, but it was *la beauté du diable*, and he was sure to come to a sinister end. And that was doubtless what had fascinated Peter, whose fascination had fascinated Denham. And there was the money, too, of course. A very pathological mix. And now Peter was involved with another young American, the third of his transatlantic paramours, who gave signs already of being bad news, having abruptly left London without explanation for Rio de Janeiro only a week or ten days before. None of this was in the least consoling to Hansen, who had been happy in London and felt no yearning to return to obscurity in America. Peter, to be sure, was understanding and generous, but even a prince may in the throes of passion be found wanting on the count of self-denying benevolence. Sonia felt sorry for Waldemar, and they remained on friendly terms always, but it was plain that her adoration for Peter took precedence even over her admiration for Cyril. She could criticize the brilliant, lazy, corpulent critic, his patron never. Waldemar voyaged homeward, I think, before I returned to Paris, and it was probably all to the good that he put behind him the ambivalence of Palace Gate.

During my fortnight in London I didn't merely attend parties and meet interesting people. I did plenty of sightseeing. And those were days when it was unmitigated delight to visit museums, cathedrals, and palaces. The tourist tidal wave was as yet an inconceivable catastrophe. How well I recall, for example, climbing up to the drawing department of the British Museum and asking whether I might see some drawings by Leonardo da Vinci. "Certainly, sir," said an elderly custodian seated behind a desk at the entrance to a vast room where tables and chairs were set in orderly ranks. "Just sign the book, please." I signed my name, nothing more, and the custodian invited me to take a seat at one of the tables. I was quite alone in that long, rather dim room. Presently the custodian brought forth a large leather portfolio, placing it before me on the table before returning to his desk. So I was left all by myself to examine the contents of the portfolio: about thirty magnificent drawings of various different subjects by Leonardo. I stayed for an hour, one of the most thrilling I have ever known. Those incomparable masterpieces, if only for one hour—in terms of rapport with beauty, an eternity—were mine alone. I possessed them, and was possessed by them, utterly. When finished, I closed the portfolio, went to the custodian's desk, and thanked him. As if my visit were a matter of routine, he nodded and said, "Good afternoon." Such an experience today would seem like the dream of a madman.

When I went back to Paris, I felt that my life had taken a momentous turn. It had, as a matter of fact, though decades were to pass before the turn led to much of a destination.

Peter came to Paris a month later. He invited me to dinner. The last issue of *Horizon* was being prepared. In addition to my story, it would include an essay on Francis Bacon by Robert Melville, with reproductions of his work, and a brilliant piece on the Marquis de Sade by Maurice Blanchot. Peter didn't seem much concerned by the demise of the review he had enthusiastically underwritten a decade before. What most preoccupied him now was the erratic behavior of his new American boyfriend, Norman Fowler, whom he was planning to follow to Rio, hoping to persuade him to give up the job he had taken as clerk in a bookstore and return to London. I didn't say so but felt that it would be far more sensible to test the boyfriend's mettle and sincerity by waiting out at home his capricious flight to Brazil. Obsessions, however, are not responsive to common sense, and Peter's was fatal.

The final issue of *Horizon* appeared early in January, containing my story, the publication of which pleased me and delighted my parents. Sonia came over to Paris in February. She was out of sorts and at loose ends. Only a few weeks after the demise of *Horizon* had come the not expected death of George Orwell. It so happened that during her visit, which was not lengthy, I was confined to bed with the flu in my small room at the Hotel Cayré. Visiting a bedridden friend so soon after the death of someone it had been necessary to visit daily in hospital for several months was unlikely, I thought, to lighten a heavy heart. But Sonia came several times, sat on a chair beside my bed, and chatted amicably. She was quite candid about Orwell's final weeks, admitted that it had often been a trial for her to keep him company, so she had sometimes neglected to stay by him when she knew he wished her to, and now felt remorseful for her failure. She was by nature impatient, she acknowledged, a serious shortcoming, and could sometimes, especially after having drunk a bit too much, give way to impetuous fits of bad temper. She never did so with me, though in years to come I heard numerous reports of embarrassing outbursts elsewhere. She was worried about Peter and missed him greatly. He and Cyril had been at the center of her life for years, and now both of them were romantically involved with people she regarded with disdain and mistrust, Peter with Fowler, Cyril with the rackety Barbara Skelton, former mistress of King Farouk. Sonia remained intimate with both of them, of course, but the intimacy now entailed unwelcome elements. Peter had not even been present to oversee the departure from Bedford Square, and

Cyril had been characteristically lazy about assuming much responsibility for the termination of his grandest enterprise. She
had had to make many important decisions by herself. The furniture was sent to storage, books and back issues were given
away or abandoned, and the files, which must have contained
material of the first importance, were left to an uncertain fate. I
asked about the Giacometti chandelier. Oh, nobody had wanted
that, Sonia said, so it was simply left hanging where we had
installed it three months before. Many years later it was saved
from permanent loss when John Craxton's infallible eye spotted
it in the out-of-the-way stall of a junk dealer who had no idea
what it was. And now that everybody save John is dead, it hangs
in the large music room at 14 Kidderpore Avenue.

Peter returned to London and kept himself busy arranging
exhibitions at the Institute for Contemporary Art, which he had
helped to found in 1947. Fowler soon followed him and moved
into the apartment at Palace Gate. Cyril married Miss Skelton,
but lack of steady employment and access to *Horizon*'s cash box
compelled him to abandon Sussex Place and go to live in a small,
unkempt country cottage owned by Barbara in Kent, where the
newlyweds quarreled continuously. Sonia's editorial talents were
soon solicited by a recently founded publishing firm called Weidenfeld and Nicolson.

I spent the summer of 1950 with my friend Bernard Minoret
in a small apartment at Villefranche-sur-Mer, then a picturesque
fishing port five miles east of Nice. It was there that we ran into
Peter and for the first time met Norman. They were also vacationing on the Riviera but in much grander accommodations.
We saw them a number of times. Peter was as charming as ever
and seemed happy with the youthful boyfriend, some twenty
years his junior, but Norman, though apparently content, did
not possess his lover's charm or princely good manners. He was
pleasant, could sometimes be good company, especially after a
few drinks, and yet a brooding, almost surly side to his nature

occasionally made his presence discomfiting. Still, with a handsome, sensual face and tall, slender, muscular physique, he was definitely an attractive man and at his best in a bathing suit. Nothing that so passionately interested Peter, however, appeared in the least to concern Norman. Bernard and I wondered what they could possibly find to talk about when alone together. I told Peter about my visits to Picasso and he responded with lively curiosity, asking well-considered questions about the artist's works in progress, while Norman gazed across the air as if all by himself in a wilderness. The four of us traveled back together to Paris by train on September 15, Norman at his moodiest during the long, tedious trip.

In October, Peter turned up alone in Paris, in search of some material for an exhibition at the Institute for Contemporary Art. He astonished me by announcing that Norman had taken it into his head to become a sculptor and was irritably complaining of the limited space in the apartment at Palace Gate, which contained, in fact, a single bedroom, a larger living room with a dining area, bath and kitchen. For a man of Peter's means it was, indeed, spartan. But Peter liked it. Norman didn't; he wanted a house in the country offering adequate space for the sculptures he aspired to create. So Peter said with a sigh that he would have to look for something. And he did look. He looked and looked but found nothing that seemed quite right. So Norman's creative ambition was frustrated and one may assume that his innate restlessness and discontent were proportionately aggravated. I saw him again but a few times the following summer, when Bernard and I, Peter and Norman once more spent some weeks in the South of France, and it appeared plain to me then that Norman was decidedly not a person easy to get along with. Peter, though, seemed wholly devoted to him and the willing servant, if not the actual accomplice, of his moody whims. So far as I know, Norman never again visited France.

It was the following February that Peter worked his magic for me when I wandered one evening into the Café des Deux-Magots and he was seated there with a bushy-haired man of about fifty, the sculptor Alberto Giacometti. After introducing me to the artist, Peter invited me to join them, and it was that meeting which altered my life completely. I have written about this at length elsewhere, but it cannot be said too often, I think, that to know Alberto at all well was inevitably to see the world and its inhabitants in a wonderfully transformed perspective, of which a passionate commitment to truth was the essential feature. Alberto painted two portraits of Peter, a tribute to that connoisseur of integrity.

Sonia was more often in Paris than Peter. She had a variety of friends there, foremost among them the French author Marguerite Duras, not yet a famous personage. I also knew Marguerite and for some years was very responsive to her charm. Though short, she was pretty, had a vibrant voice and a persuasive conviction of her importance. An avowed member of the French Communist Party, the most Stalinist in the West, she frequently delivered anti-American harangues which seemed to me quite as laughable as those of Picasso, and, in any case, she was later excluded from the Party as a consequence of too overt pursuit of male comrades. In the sixties she made a French adaptation of the play I had written based on Henry James's great novella, *The Beast in the Jungle*. Fame did not agree with Marguerite. She became querulous, avaricious, drank to excess, and lost most of her old friends. But in those early years with Sonia her company was stimulating and delightful.

In 1951 and 1952 I wrote a novel, by no means my first effort in that genre. But this one, I felt, had a little more substance than the others. Perhaps it seemed better because I believed it to be not at all autobiographical, whereas in fact it was based very closely on my youthful and self-indulgent experiences. Remembering Sonia's capable assistance with my story and aware that she was now an editor in a publishing house, I sent the

manuscript to London. It was accepted by Weidenfeld and Nicolson, but Sonia wrote that it could be much improved by ju-
dicious reworking and generously offered her assistance. So it
came about that in the summer of 1954, while I was staying
with Dora Maar in Provence, I drove over the mountains to the
Riviera, where I found Sonia and a friend named Janetta Jackson
staying in a picturesque house lodged in the ramparts of Haut-
de-Cagnes. The three of us had a very jolly time together. Janetta was an exceptionally talented cook and we drank a good
deal of iced vin rosé. Sonia went over the entire manuscript with
me, making many wise suggestions for revision, all of which I
prudently followed, and on the basis of the English publication
the novel later appeared in America as well. But it was a mediocre piece of work, one which would never find a publisher
today. I like to forget it, though the memory of Sonia's friendly
and efficient helping hand remains bright.

Bad news, fortunately, sometimes travels at a snail's pace. It
was not until early June in 1956 that I learned of Peter's death.
Sonia told me all the details, and they were bizarre. As an introduction to that year, Peter had at last found a new residence
which was to his taste, not a house in the country where Norman
could create sculptures, but a spacious flat in Rutland Gate. Anyway, if Norman ever created a single sculpture, nobody knew of
it. One day in the first week of May, Peter had been found dead,
drowned in his bath in the new flat. The circumstances were
suspicious. Though it was true that he had not always been in
the best of health, having suffered from jaundice and anemia,
his heart was strong and recently he had been in the best of
humors, preparing a new exhibition for the ICA. He was only
forty-eight years old and over six feet in height. That such a man
could drown in his bath seemed, to say the least, peculiar. Moreover, at the time of his death he had not been alone in the flat.
Norman was there. The police were immediately suspicious. The
young man was his older lover's principal heir, and a large

amount of money was involved. There was an inquest. Norman's story was that he and Peter had had a violent argument over some trifle, which Peter had terminated by going into the bathroom and slamming the door. Norman claimed that he had remained in the bedroom and fallen asleep. But is sleep, one wonders, a normal reaction to a violent argument? In any event, at the inquest he contended that he had awakened some time later, gone to the bathroom door, found it locked from the inside and water flowing out from beneath it. Something was obviously wrong. The young man, he asserted, had immediately run out into the street in search of a police officer, who returned with him to the flat, broke open the bathroom door, and found Peter in the tub, the taps still running, his head underwater, dead. But why, one wonders again, did Norman not break into the bathroom himself if he had had nothing to fear from the sight of water running under the door except that some plumbing mishap might have occurred? Why did he go in search specifically of a police officer when time might have been decisive? Would not the very first passerby—or even a neighbor in the building—have provided help enough? A police officer, to be sure, if ever foul play were suspected, would have provided more authoritative evidence. It was the fact that the bathroom door was locked from the inside that made all the difference. Is it not possible, however, that a skillful tinkerer could manage from the outside to lock a door as if from the inside? But the coroner's verdict was that Peter's death had been accidental. Many people, including Sonia and myself, felt disinclined to agree. Fowler was a neurotic, bad-tempered young man, and letters written while he was living with Peter which came to light many years later reveal a morbid fascination with violent death.

Norman, in any case, inherited almost everything, a great deal of money and all the very valuable works of art. Sonia was left two thousand pounds, Cyril one. When the estate was settled, the heir showed how much care he had actually felt for the feelings and interests of his defunct benefactor, because the very first items of Peter's property that he sold were all his private papers, the letters and manuscripts of countless writers, artists, and musicians who had been his friends and admirers, many of them famous men whose unpublished writings brought high prices from dealers in such material. Sonia raged against the heartless vulgarity of this act, and people who had been polite to Norman for Peter's sake turned their backs on him. But he didn't linger long in London. Taking with him Peter's cash and works of art, he went to live in the Virgin Islands, where he idly spent his time sailing and fishing. He sold the works of art to a New York dealer named Patti Birch, who bought them at low prices, including an anonymous seventeenth-century picture that Peter had bought simply because he liked it but which turned out to be a Poussin, posthumous testimony to Peter's unerring eye for the best—save in lovers. But the bizarre workings of fate which had presided over Fowler's relation to Peter and his behavior at the time of Peter's death held an even stranger twist in store for the unfeeling recipient of so much largesse. Eventually he bought a small hotel on the tiny island of Nevis. It was named the Bath Hotel, because it offered a number of large hot-water baths in which guests could seek relief from rheumatism or other ailments. In one of these, early in 1971, Norman Fowler was found dead by drowning. He was forty-four, just four years younger than Peter at the time of his death in exactly the same manner fourteen years before. There was suspicion of foul play. Fowler was not a man who went out of his way to make himself liked. But no evidence was brought forward to support a charge of murder, and Norman's death, like Peter's, was officially held to have been accidental.

Sonia had been tearful when she first told me of our friend's death and the sinister cremation ceremony at Golders Green. She often spoke of Peter. There was no doubt that she had loved him, as numerous people had. There aren't so many of us remaining now to remember him, but for those who do, I think, his memory is something like the odor of faded peonies in a beautiful room that has been uninhabited for decades, the blinds drawn, dust sheets thrown over the rare furniture. And someday before very long, nobody will be left at all to realize from experience how precious and generous a man was Peter Watson.

It was after Peter's death and Cyril's decline into marital desperation and necessitous journalism that Sonia, like her friend Marguerite, took seriously to drink. When drunk, she could be loud, sometimes abusive, seriously trying the patience of old friends like Stephen and Natasha Spender, who nevertheless continued to see her. She was not an outright alcoholic, not yet anyway, and as for myself I continued no less than before to enjoy her company, her vivacious sense of humor and serious concern for literature. People accused her of being an irrepressible intellectual snob, but I, who also sought the company of people whose talents and achievements I could admire, did not find reason to fault her on that score.

In 1958 Sonia surprised her friends by announcing that she intended to marry. Their surprise became astonishment, almost consternation, when she revealed the identity of her fiancé. Having sat at the feet of Cyril, arguably the most eminent man of letters of his generation, and paraded her adoration of Peter, she now proposed to become the wife of a man who had no literary or artistic leanings whatever. He was by no means unknown, however. A few years before he had been one of the two defendants in a notorious trial, on charges of having had indecent relations with some underage Boy Scouts, an offense of which both men were found guilty and for which they were sentenced to eighteen months' imprisonment. The Scouts, incidentally, were rumored to have been quite willing to participate in indecency for a modest monetary consideration and it was said that the authorities were zealous in prosecution of the case principally because the men involved were gentlemen of distinction, one of them, indeed, an eminent young member of the House of Lords. Victorian prudery was still keen to make examples of prominent persons who, like Oscar Wilde, flouted it, while the lower classes had little to worry about. Imprisonment in the fifties was no longer the brutal affliction that destroyed Wilde, but it was no joke, and the scandal was great. Sonia's fiancé was not the young, haughty lord but a personable, attractive member of a highly distinguished and very rich family. His name: Michael Pitt-Rivers. He happened to be the grandson of the British general who had commanded the force which in 1897 conquered and burned the capital city of the ancient African kingdom of Benin, destroying much of the country's splendid and treasured art, some of it dating from the thirteenth century and considered by many connoisseurs to be the finest ever produced in Africa. General Pitt-Rivers, however, was able to plunder and take back with him to England a large quantity of the bronze plaques, portrait busts, and carved ivories which had been the glory of the ancient city. With the passing of time and a growing appreciation of African art, this loot amounted to a very valuable collection, most of which was sold by Michael's father. Michael's principal claim to personal distinction was the fact, very greatly to his credit, that he had survived the ordeal of imprisonment with his good humor, good manners, and cultivated charm intact. Some people said that Sonia may have been prepared to marry him for snobbish and material reasons, but I rather believe it was his homosexuality, like Peter's, that made him seem acceptable, as it would have been likely to obviate serious, unwelcome emotional commitment.

The wedding, in any case, was celebrated in becoming style. One wonders what Michael's relatives can have thought of Sonia. Doubtless, they were overjoyed to see the ex-convict married, but for them his bride was something of a bohemian, accustomed to associating with authors and artists, and the gentry knew just what they thought of the propriety of such people.

Any misgivings they may have felt proved in time—and not a very long time, either—to be only too well founded.

The newlyweds soon came over to Paris, where Sonia was eager to present her husband to the very friends of whom his relatives were most likely to disapprove. We found him charming, good-looking, and very politely bent upon making himself liked by everyone introduced to him by his wife. One lovely warm Sunday, Sonia, Michael, Bernard, and I drove out in my car to a pleasant little town about twenty-five miles away called Les Mesnuls to have lunch at La Toque Blanche, a well-known restaurant, where we lingered long over the delectable food and excellent wines. All were in the best of spirits, laughing over idle gossip, exchanging anecdotes, and happily talking about movies and Marguerite and the latest books and exhibitions and parties. Michael was very easy to like. It was that day, however, that I first observed Sonia drinking more than she should have. She started talking stridently and far too loud, and when we finally left the restaurant to stroll about the town in the gleaming afternoon, she was somewhat unsteady on her feet. It seemed to me that Michael looked ill at ease, with creases of worry around the eyes, but I may have been mistaken.

I wasn't, as I found out the following December, when I spent ten days in England. Michael owned a country house on the family estate in Wiltshire, not far from Salisbury, an ancient, tall, rather austere stone building called King John's House because it had had some connection with that belligerent monarch, whose principal claim to remembrance is that he was compelled to sign the Magna Charta, the most famous document in British history and symbol of the supremacy of the constitution over the king. Sonia invited me to come down there for a weekend and I gladly agreed. The weather was mild for mid-December. We drove over to Salisbury to view the cathedral with its magnificent spire so beloved by Constable. Before dinner, drinks were served in a grand drawing room. On a table before the fireplace I noticed a fine bronze of a female figure by Giacometti, a middle-sized piece of the mid-fifties, one of the most refined creations from a period judged by many critics to have been the most accomplished of the sculptor's career. It had been Michael's wedding present, Sonia said, selected, needless to add, by herself. She was very proud of it, especially as she had met the artist in the home of one of Giacometti's oldest friends, Michel Leiris, a man who had many acquaintances in the English art world, including Francis Bacon, Lucian Freud, the critic David Sylvester, Giacometti's sometime mistress Isabel Rawsthorne, and Sonia herself, to name but a few. She caressed the figure lovingly, asserting that it was her most precious possession, one with which she would never part, swaying slightly as she declared her passion for the sculpture and admiration for its creator. She had had several drinks by this time. Dinner and wine were still to come. Michael, I observed, watched his wife with conspicuous concern. The only other guest was a large lady named Véra Russell, the former wife of the art critic John Russell, a man later to have a prominent career in America. Véra was a shrewd and imposing personality, never one to mince words or opinions. Glancing at Sonia, who was fondling the Giacometti, then at me, she raised her eyebrows and shook her head very slightly but eloquently enough. I looked away. During dinner, helped in candor by superb claret, Sonia told stories of her childhood in India. I never on any other occasion heard her mention it and noticed that not a word was said about her mother, who may at that time have still been living. Sonia's family consisted exclusively of her literary and artist friends.

Though a cultivated gentleman to his fingertips and sociability personified, Michael could hardly have been considered either literary or artistic. He didn't write or paint. Neither had Peter, for that matter, but his life was concentrated very much on those who did. Michael's life was not. The Giacometti bronze was the only object in King John's House to suggest that its inhabitant was much concerned by contemporary culture. It was in that house that I first began to suspect that the marriage had been on both sides drastically ill-considered and was fated to end badly. Events of the next few days added much to my suspicion.

To luncheon on the Sunday, Michael had invited three neighboring couples, ladies and gentlemen, two of them considerably older, who could have served very nicely as models of county gentlefolk for *Pride and Prejudice*. I can't think what led him to be so rash. It seems inconceivable that he might have imagined his wife would be found agreeable—even, perhaps, presentable—to such a decorous group or that she, indeed, would take pains to make herself welcome. As we stood about drinking champagne in the drawing room before luncheon, Véra murmured to me that this comedy was not going to be amusing. She was right. Well before we were summoned to the dining room, our hostess was noticeably tipsy. Ten people at a long, rectangular table should have produced several separate conversations. This proved for the most part impossible because Sonia, seated at the head of the table, insistently talked in a louder and louder voice to Véra and me about the Leirises, Marguerite Duras, Lacan, André Masson, and other people of whom her guests had never heard and who in all likelihood, even if they had, would not have been welcomed in polite society. Pursed lips and empty eyes were eloquent testimony to unexpressed thoughts. Michael was clearly pained and several times endeavored to stem the onrush of Sonia's chatter by talking to his neighbors, but he never managed to sustain a conversation because she kept on talking while gulping her wine, and the husband was not going to engage in a shouting match with his wife. The guests departed in a chilly mist of *politesse* very soon after coffee. And not much later a car came to fetch Véra and me for the train trip back to London. Our thanks and farewells may have given away a surge of relief at being spared the confrontation between husband and wife when finally alone together.

En route in the train, we talked about Sonia. My companion, that is, talked about her. Véra, of whom I was to see a good deal in years to come, Russian by birth, was a willful and outspoken woman who had seen and understood much. I was a stranger to her at the time, but she spoke to me as candidly about our weekend hostess as though we were already firm friends. She had known Sonia, she said, from the beginning, that being her appearance aged only about twenty among a group of unknown young painters who were attracted by her beauty and painted portraits of her. Through them she became acquainted with Stephen Spender, then dabbling in painting himself, and through Stephen with Cyril Connolly, Peter Watson, and the *Horizon* milieu. Connolly in particular had been strongly drawn to her, but she evaded his amorous maneuvers. Véra thought there had always been a powerful though, perhaps, latent lesbian drive in Sonia's nature. What had been deeply harmful to her in the long run, Véra conjectured, was her stubborn, even obsessive determination to become a person who counted for much in the literary and artistic world, because she lacked the intellectual power and spiritual stamina necessary to attain and then to maintain with authority and serenity any such position. The proof of this was the fact that the one true love affair of her life had been with the French philosopher Maurice Merleau-Ponty, which had been brief and ended badly for the simple reason that Sonia was in no way equipped to cope with the intellectual or psychic challenge of intimacy with such a man. The subsequent marriage to Orwell had been a serious mistake, because it had merely given her a name to nourish the illusion of deserving alliance to great literary achievement. She was a romantic without the emotional resilience to make romance the mainstay of her life. Her most passionate desire was to become a symbolic figure, which she had never had the wherewithal to be. This was what others found puzzling about her, which led occasionally to outrageous behavior, while at the same time she remained essentially kind and pure at heart. In short, Sonia was a woman who would never be at peace with herself and would consequently be unable to provide it for anyone else. And yet she remained unusually likable, a strangely contradictory individual. It was a pity, said Véra, by way of conclusion, that instead of getting mixed up in the Connolly–Watson–Bacon–Freud world she hadn't married a millionaire from the City, gone to Covent Garden, Wimbledon, and Ascot and arranged lavish dinner parties for Rockefellers and Rothschilds.

A couple of days later, Michael and Sonia being in London, they invited me to go with them to a cocktail party at the house of some people I didn't know. They picked me up at Brown's in Michael's car. It was raining. On the way to the party, which was in a crescent somewhere beyond the V and A, we had to make another stop to take along a couple who were friends of Sonia but unknown either to me or to Michael. They were young and attractive but rather reserved. Sonia, who was sitting in front beside her husband, turned round to make the introductions, presented me as an American author, then gave Michael's name, adding, "Oh yes, he's the one who was in prison for buggery." That stunningly gratuitous statement of fact reduced to tense silence the remainder of the ride to the party. Sonia was already drunk, of course. Still, I couldn't help feeling outraged at the infliction of such pointless humiliation, if not keen pain. Luckily, the rain soon stopped. I was able to make my departure without saying goodbye to anyone. I never saw Michael again.

Some time passed, then in the early sixties I was seeing a good deal of La Du-du, as we called Marguerite Duras, for she was fiddling in her inimitable, often irritating way with my French version of the play adapted from Henry James's story. And Sonia was often in Paris. The marriage with Michael had miraculously enough been ended amicably, and was the terminal emotional entanglement of her life. Both she and La Du-du were drinking heavily during this period, and it was now that Sonia began to deserve to be described as a "difficult woman." But she was always sociable and gaily talkative with me, even when drunk. It's true that with Sonia I was lucky. We had lunch or dinner together a number of times, and she would ramble on with sad or joyful nostalgia about the wonderful years of *Horizon*'s glory. Her veneration for Cyril never wavered, though his great days were long gone, and she spoke of Peter with lachrymose devotion. No mention of Michael. In her early forties, she looked well past fifty, the Renoir beauty of her youth having worn away. Even so, she seemed to face the future with confident enthusiasm.

During the mid-sixties, having moved temporarily to New York, I saw next to nothing of Sonia. It was then that she came to live in Paris, took a small apartment at 38, rue des Saints-Pères, and set about launching a review which she must have hoped would become a worthy successor to the one that had been so wondrous in her youth. Financed by her friend Anne Dunn, daughter of a millionaire banker, it was called *Art and Literature*, a patent, presumably enticing echo of the subtitle to *Horizon*. Sonia was not the sole editor, being assisted by Anne Dunn and her painter husband, Rodrigo Moynihan, and, more important, by the highly talented American poet and critic John Ashbery, then also resident in Paris. *Art and Literature* managed to gather an appreciable harvest of prestige, but it did not appear as regularly as *Horizon* and never came close to the imposing summits of quality scaled with such lackadaisical discrimination by Cyril. Its life was only half as long, its demise regarded by few as an occasion for mourning. But it must be said that in the forty-five years since *Horizon* expired no other periodical has come close to matching its empyrean standards of excellence.

Throughout the early seventies, once more resident in Paris, I went on several occasions to London to pursue research for the biography of Alberto Giacometti, which I had rashly under-

taken to write. I called Sonia, arranging to dine with her. At the
appointed time she neither appeared nor telephoned to explain
her absence. The next day I called again only to be told in a
very offhand manner that she had been indisposed and couldn't
make it. I said that I hoped to see her soon nonetheless but
specifically neglected to set a date. And that, I thought, was
perhaps that. But it wasn't.

An art dealer in Paris named Claude Bernard whom I've
known for many years owns a luxurious estate in Touraine, complete with chapel, vast greenhouses, a Moroccan patio, and a
private theater seating five hundred. He has sometimes invited
me to spend weekends there, and it was during the last weekend
of April in 1977 that I found Sonia to be one of the other
guests. To my great surprise and even greater pleasure, she
seemed to be almost the long-ago Sonia of happier, younger
years and even shone now and then with traces of the beauty
once so radiantly hers. She drank with noticeable moderation,
never once appearing to have had too much. The Sunday was
glorious, a warm sun highlighting tender greens, lilacs, and the
first tiny golden wildflowers in roadside ditches. After lunch
Sonia and I went for a walk together along the narrow, uphill
road and across fields just reawakening to fertility. Having
known each other for almost thirty years, we seemed to discover
only then that we were old and affectionate friends. We talked
of the many people we had known together, the enthusiasms we
had shared, the ups and downs of destinies, any number of
gleaming memories. She was justly proud, and said so, of having
co-edited the four-volume *Collected Essays, Journalism and Letters of George Orwell*, an imposing testimony to her self-control,
her energy, and the genius of her short-lived husband. It was a
wonder, our rambling talk, and I didn't try to record it in detail
later, only dwelling upon the surprise and pleasure. When we
got back to the house, it was time to take to our separate cars
for the return to Paris. Sonia and I promised each other with

honest eagerness to meet again the next time I came to London.

That was two years later, in mid-June. I called Sonia (Free-mantle 1559) at her house in Gloucester Road. We agreed to have lunch the following day, a Thursday. At about quarter to one, I went to the house, No. 153, an unimposing three-story building in very moderate repair, its yellow paint peeling, win-dowpanes grimy, and front steps cracked. I rang the clanging old-fashioned bell. It was several minutes before the door opened very slowly, as if great effort were needed to make it move. And there she stood, a gray-haired woman in a stained dressing gown, staring out at me. To say that I wouldn't have recognized her would be absurd, because she was the person I'd expected to see. It was certainly Sonia. But on a crowded street at noon I'm not sure I would have known the person I remem-bered as Sonia. Her face was pudgy and wrinkled, hair in a tangle, eyes pink and vague. And it was not at all obvious that she recognized me.

"Oh," she murmured after a moment, "it's you, Jim. Well then, come in, I suppose."

She led the way into a long room with windows opening to-ward the street and an unkempt bit of garden in the rear. It had not been cleaned for some time. The overstuffed furniture, of indeterminate color, was in desperate disrepair. She sat down with her back to the light. On the table beside her, I saw a glass half filled. Behind the sofa, two empty gin bottles lay on the floor. Glancing about in search of the Giacometti sculpture, I didn't see it and forbore to inquire, but I learned later from the dealer who bought it that she had sold it some years before and that it had been broken in two places, damage difficult to repair. I stood there ill at ease, not knowing what to say or try to do. I had hoped to take her to luncheon at Wheeler's in Old Comp-ton Street, where we had so often happily eaten in the past with Peter, John, and Lucian, but I realized that this was impossible.

"You shouldn't have come," said Sonia.

"But we agreed," I said.

"I know, I know." She sighed. "I always agree. But don't you see? You should never have come. It's impossible now. Too late."

"I'm sorry," I said.

"That's no good," she exclaimed wearily. "Everybody's sorry."

"Well, then I guess I'd better run along," I said. "But the next time I'm in London I'll call."

"By all means," said Sonia, "do ring me by all means." She waved her hand. It was a gesture of farewell.

I would have liked to give her a kiss to say goodbye, as I'd often done in the past, but I recognized that that would be presumptuous now. Indeed, it *was* too late. So I said goodbye, waved in response to her farewell, and went out. She did not make a move to accompany me.

Walking back to the main thoroughfare in search of a taxi, I thought of the innocent days three decades before, the cozy flat in Percy Street, the parties at Cyril's and Peter's, the aspirations and expectations, the merry-go-round of the literary life. For Sonia, as for so many, it had all come to this, after the champagne at the Ritz, after the fame of Mrs. Orwell, after the dedication and hard work and powerful illusions, after the tea with T. S. Eliot, after all, it had come to this: a woman aged before her time, lonely, drunken, and bereft. Véra's cold-blooded analysis had been all too accurate. Sonia had never possessed the wherewithal to become the person, the only person, she passionately desired to become.

Toward the end of the following year she died, aged only sixty-two.

Part Five

A FIREFLY IN THE MEADOW

ETHEL BLISS PLATT

The Blisses lived in a large white house. It was separated from the flagstone sidewalk of Engle Street by broad lawns and a white picket fence. In short, it stood apart, and so did the Blisses. Every town, no matter how obscure, boasts and needs its share of aristocrats. Like the Lydeckers, the Platts, the Paysons, the Morrows, and the Scarboroughs, the Blisses were Englewood's nobility. I can recall seeing the house as a small child, and more than any other in the town—perhaps because of its distant simplicity and purity—it evoked a sense of fairy-tale enchantment and seemed to beckon to the innocent imagination. It was torn down along with most of Englewood's grand houses well before the pristine wonder of childhood could be spoiled by experience. Twenty-five years later I learned how supremely appropriate that unsophisticated sense of delight had been. For Ethel had been born and had grown up in that house and had driven her pony cart along unpaved streets under the mulberry trees.

My parents were not counted among Englewood's aristocrats, nor did they aspire to be. I, on the other hand, from an early age had a hankering for things aristocratic. This, however, had nothing to do with the *Almanach de Gotha*, of which I had never heard, or the people whose names appear between its crimson covers. The nobility I pined for got its start in my dreams when I began to haunt museums. It was art, I felt, that determined the aristocratic principle, but not the art that filled museums, because it belonged to everyone, thus to no one in particular, and therefore could not confer on a specific individual the distinction that accompanied the possession of works of art which ennobled one's home. It was familiarity with a rich and cultivated elite that I craved rather than the acquaintance of people who had no claim to eminence other than their ancestry (often illegitimate). It was in the house and among the masterpieces bequeathed as a museum to the City of New York by Henry Clay Frick that I first had an intimation of the exaltation to be experienced through intimate association with great works of art. In those halcyon days before the Second World War, when admission to the Frick Collection was free and next to nobody came, it was almost possible to imagine that one was visiting the splendid home of an acquaintance who had just stepped out for a stroll on Fifth Avenue. Almost, but not quite. There were, after all, somnolent guards and a few other visitors, and the premises, not to mention the paintings, were far too splendid to allow for a sense of private, tranquil delectation. In later years it was my luck to become familiar with people whose homes contained great works by Rembrandt, Velázquez, Goya, Degas, Cézanne, all the masters of our century, and even one Vermeer. They were the aristocrats whose acquaintance I sought. Some of them were, in fact, authentic aristocrats and lived in appropriate palaces, but candor persuades me to say that my emotions were in most cases more moved by the possessions than by their proprietors. In any case, I emphatically felt that there was greater aesthetic delight and benefit to be had from contemplating an Ingres in the quiet drawing room of a friend than from seeing Monsieur Bertin in the Louvre. It never occurred to me, though, that in Englewood, New Jersey, my birth-place, I would encounter such benefit and delight, to which might be added the close and heartfelt friendship of someone whose poignant sensitivity could actually enhance the beauty of rare works of art.

My adolescent rambles around Englewood often led me past the few grand houses that remained, and I used to gaze at their windows, wondering what marvels might possibly be secreted within. As a matter of fact, I assumed there were none, because I had been invited into a few of these houses by school friends and all I had seen was fake French and Italian furniture, dismal paintings, and ugly gewgaws. And yet, had I but known, there was in the town one house, and one only, of which the contents merited and received intoxicating admiration. It was visited, in-deed, by the great connoisseurs and collectors of the era, Mr. Morgan in person, the rapacious Lord Duveen, even hard-fisted old Frick, and many and many another. I didn't find this out, alas, until much too late. By no means one of the largest or most ostentatious of Englewood's houses, it was nonetheless of very ample size, a white building discreetly reminiscent of an Italian villa, set in spacious grounds at the corner of Booth Av-enue and Lydecker Street. I asked my parents who lived in it and was told that the inhabitants were a childless couple by the name of Platt, Dan and Ethel. My mother had met them at an afternoon reception given by Mrs. Dwight Morrow, had found Dan Platt formal and remote, Ethel pleasant but also graciously distant. They were on friendly terms with very few people in Englewood, it seemed, and did not belong to the country club, were frequently in New York, and traveled abroad for several months in the summer. This information was unfortunately in-adequate to excite my inquisitive daring. Besides, at age sixteen, how could I have tendered—even to myself—an interest suffi-ciently refined to justify an introduction to the fabulous contents of that house? So it was not really an opportunity missed, though many years later I liked to believe that the ingenuous thrill of appreciation would have been adequate.

Then came the war, and afterwards I was often back and forth between France and America. When at home, I stayed with my parents and sometimes attended the parties given by them or their friends. It so happened that one of the most eminent physicians in the United States, Dana W. Atchley, resided in Englewood and was a close friend of my mother and father. He was a man of international reputation, counting among his patients the Aga Khan, Dean Acheson, the Secretary of State, Greta Garbo, Charles Lindbergh, and many other celebrated persons as well as neighbors and friends. It was from casual remarks made by him and his wife, Mary, that my interest in the house on Booth Avenue was excitingly revived. Dan Platt, it seems, had died shortly before the war, leaving his widow to cope with the disposition of the great collection of works of art to which he had devoted his life. "What sort of collection?" I immediately inquired. Dr. Atchley didn't know much about art, and Mary knew less, but both had frequently been inside the Platts' house, had had opportunities to look over the contents, and had been awed by what they saw. There had been pictures everywhere, almost all of them Italian, not dozens but hundreds, hanging from floor to ceiling, in the hall, on the staircase, in every room downstairs and all the bedrooms, many stacked one against another on the floor, plus portfolios filled with drawings, Renaissance and Egyptian sculptures, splendid furniture, and rare carpets. It was one of the most important collections of early Italian art in America, Dana said. But what had become of it, I longed to be told. They didn't know. Ethel must have made some kind of disposition, because not long ago she had sold the mansion on Booth Avenue and had had built for herself a much smaller house on Cedar Street, where she had hanging in her living room and hallway eight or ten beautiful paintings. I determined at once to make the acquaintance of Mrs. Platt.

From Hillside Avenue, where my parents lived, to Cedar Street was but seven or eight minutes' walk. The house that interested me, number 200, was easy to distinguish from its neighbors, being clearly of recent construction and architecturally more distinguished than its neighbors, a modest but formal two-story residence of whitened brick set well back from the street, with a one-car garage to its right. The driveway was of tawny gravel, and a white gate beneath an archway led to the invisible entrance. The façade facing the street was obviously the rear of the house, which gave one to infer that the person who lived there might be unlikely to enjoy the visits of strangers. This did not deter me. I had no good reason to suppose that Mrs. Platt would be prepared to make me welcome, but from the first I had an irrational feeling that ultimately a fine, exclusive harmony could exist between myself and the elderly lady who lived in that house. It was rash and naïve, but so at thirty was I.

I wrote her a letter, explaining that I had learned of her art collection from the Atchleys and would greatly appreciate an opportunity to admire it. The reply was prompt.

> 200 Cedar Street
> 10 December 1952
>
> Dear Mr. Lord,
>
> What I have here are only remnants of the collection formed by my late husband. If it would interest you to see them I should be pleased to receive you for tea next Thursday, one week from today, at four o'clock. Kindly let me know if this will be convenient.
>
> Yours truly,
>
> E. B. Platt

I immediately replied that it would be convenient, adding that I appreciated her courtesy and looked forward with much pleasure to our meeting.

Several inches of snow lay on the ground, but a neat path had been shoveled to Mrs. Platt's gate and beyond it to the front

door. I rang at four o'clock precisely. A heavily built maid in
uniform opened the door. The entryway was small, held only a
table and chair. A large Venetian *veduta* hung above the table,
Santa Maria della Salute, rather like a Canaletto but less crisp, a
Marieschi perhaps, and on the table was a Greek female torso
of glinting marble. The maid took my coat and boots, put them
into a closet, then led me down a short corridor and indicated
a door to the left. All this without having said a single word.
Mrs. Platt came forward from a large window. "It's kind of you
to be punctual," she said.

"That's one of my defects," I replied as we shook hands.

She was as tall as I, slender, with ash-gray hair cut close to
her head, a large mouth and few wrinkles, pale gray eyes that
candidly inspected her visitor. She wore almost no makeup, only
the slightest touch of pink on the lips. Her carriage was of ineffable distinction, and she did not appear disposed to put one
at ease. It seemed evident at once that if any ice were to be
broken between us I would have to make the first crack. "You
are very kind to allow me to come."

She gestured to an armchair on the far side of a low Italian
table and said, "Do sit down. Netty will serve us tea in a moment." She took the matching armchair on the other side of the
table. A silence ensued, permitting me to glance at the walls.
Above a marquetry desk by the door hung a beautiful Nativity
of brilliant warmth and remarkable rendering of individual character, slightly reminiscent of van der Goes. Above the fireplace
was a large painting of a kneeling angel with gold hair and a
green gown holding a flambeau. "That's a Bernardino Luini,"
said Mrs. Platt. "A fragment of a fresco from a villa near Milan.
Luini was very close to Leonardo, as you probably are aware. It
was one of the very first pictures purchased by Dan Platt."

"It's very beautiful," I inadequately murmured.

"I'll never part with it," she said.

Lower down on the wall to the right of the fireplace hung a

portrait head of a very handsome youth with long hair and round bonnet, apparently Venetian, reminiscent of Bellini but more gentle and sensuous. There were other paintings but I couldn't see them from where I sat. Then the maid brought in our tea on a large silver tray, the matching service of fragile, nearly transparent porcelain decorated with ladybugs, butterflies, and golden wasps. She set this down on the table between us, went out, and returned with a silver salver laden with tawny slices of fruitcake. Mrs. Platt poured tea with queenly ease, inquiring about sugar, milk—not cream!—or lemon, handed me my cup and then a matching plate with a slice of cake and a filmy, lace-embroidered napkin. That she had been doing this all her life was exquisitely obvious, and I felt rather like one of the insects painted on my teacup. As we sipped and nibbled there was another long silence, stretching trackless over the unbroken ice, and I wondered whether it might not be simpler to drink my tea and leave. Anyway, the pictures, though very beautiful, were not nearly so overwhelming as the hostess.

"I presume," she said at last, "that you are a student of art history."

"No. I'm just very interested. I've never actually studied art history. I hope I haven't been too presumptuous, inviting myself to your home. The Atchleys, you see, are friends of my parents, and from them I learned that you had a collection. It's unexpected in Englewood."

She replied that I was not in the least presumptuous. When Dan Platt was living, people had come constantly to see the pictures. Then, of course, there were many more. Oh, so many more. But if I was not a student of art history, she inquired, what did I do? I explained with embarrassment that I was trying to become a writer, had written several novels but so far had met with no success. She told me not to worry about that. "Leonardo warned against it," she said.

Another silence ensued. Mrs. Platt gazed out the window at

her snow-covered yard, which was divided in two horizontally by a split-rail fence. She seemed to be musing about some perplexing issue. I did not feel that it was my prerogative to intervene. At length she murmured, "Santayana. I don't imagine anyone reads him today, although he died only recently. We sometimes visited him in Italy. Dan Platt was a great admirer of *The Realms of Being*. Have you read him?"

I told her that I'd tried *The Last Puritan* but found it didn't hold my interest.

"He's better about Erasmus," said Mrs. Platt.

Outside, it was now growing dark. My hostess stood up and turned on some lamps. "There really aren't many pictures. This is a Vittorio Crivelli, St. Anthony of Padua." It hung above a small table beside a door leading outside, a panel painting of good size on gold ground of a bald monk holding a branch of lilies. "And here is a Taddeo di Bartolo of St. Anthony Abbott and St. Ansano." There were two large panels in a gilt Gothic tabernacle, which must originally have been part of an important altarpiece. Another panel of the Virgin and Child in very bad condition hung on a side wall by the deep bay window where a table and chairs were arranged, apparently for dining. "We called her the ruined Madonna," said Mrs. Platt, "and that's about all. Oh, there's a fragment by Tiepolo in the hall, a drawing by Blake, and a couple of Romneys in the guest room."

The Tiepolo was a painting in gouache on linen, a study of a woman's head, very beautiful though much of the paint had flaked off. The Blake was of a nude male blowing a trumpet. The Romneys were quick ink sketches of Lady Hamilton. The picture I admired most was the Venetian portrait of the handsome youth. I also felt impressed by the remnants of Tiepolo's quicksilver mastery. Both of these pictures hang in my living room in Paris today. Ethel has been dead for twenty-five years, but I have no need of them to remember her. By the front door hung a tiny ink drawing of a mouse. "Salvator Rosa," she said.

And that was the end of my first visit to Cedar Street. As I was putting on my boots she said, "If you come back sometime, we can talk about Emily Dickinson."

I said that she was one of my favorites, but this brought no response. We shook hands and I went out into the snow-white darkness, reflecting that not once during my visit, which had lasted little more than an hour, had Mrs. Platt smiled. A regal air certainly surrounded her, also an aura of self-possessed solitude. I assumed that my first visit was likely to be the last. But I may be forgiven for being so obtuse, because the only way to know Ethel was to pay very close attention to her merest intimation. This was not easy. It was wonderfully worthwhile, however.

Christmas passed. I was then making preliminary arrangements for raising money to preserve Cézanne's studio in Aix-en-Provence. This kept me busy. Mrs. Platt was not on my mind. She called me on the telephone, suggesting that if I would like to come to her house for a drink that very afternoon she'd enjoy having me read a poem aloud. It was the sort of impromptu invitation impossible to refuse.

She met me herself at the door and carefully put away my winter attire in her hall closet. I sat in the same armchair by the window. It was always to be in that same armchair that I sat save on those rare occasions when we lunched together at the table in the farther window. Everything in the room seemed changeless. Even after the pictures—all except the Luini angel —were gone, I never felt that the room had radically been altered. That was because Ethel herself remained so supremely as she was. On the Italian table between our two armchairs, a book of poetry lay open. She pointed to a poem of four stanzas on the left-hand page and said that that was the one she would be pleased to have me read. I told her that I had had little experience in reading aloud, but she said, "I'm not expecting eloquence." So I read the poem.

There's a certain slant of light,
Winter afternoons—
That oppresses, like the heft
Of cathedral tunes.

Heavenly hurt it gives us—
We can find no scar,
But internal difference,
Where the meanings are.

None may teach it—any—
'Tis the seal despair—
An imperial affliction
Sent us of the air.

When it comes, the landscape listens,
Shadows hold their breath—
When it goes, 'tis like the distance
On the look of death.

"Thank you," said my hostess. "That was quite eloquent enough. I won't ask you to read another. Not today, that is. Maybe when the meadow is in bloom. You know, she saw very deep and very far just looking out her window in Amherst. That's not what I'd call being a recluse, the whole world lying at the point of her pen. This is a winter afternoon like that. Like the distance on the look of death. We used to go to Europe every year, Dan Platt and I. And then when we came back just before the second war broke out, he said in the car as we were driving home, he said, 'Effie, I feel a dark shadow over me.' And a few weeks afterward he was gone. It was a winter afternoon." I learned later that he'd been only sixty-five years old. She gazed out the window at the shadows, which indeed appeared to be holding their breath, gathering silent darkness from the bare black trees.

I felt stricken. This was not at all what I had expected. But then, as if we had been discussing a tennis tournament, Ethel said it was time for a drink. She took sherry, I Scotch. And during that visit, only the second of an uncounted number during the succeeding twenty years, I sensed that I would probably never know another intimacy as profound, robust, and queenly as hers. To be sure, I had not yet made the acquaintance of Errieta,* and though the two women's lives could hardly have been less alike, both were imbued by exceptional strength of character and true constancy of feeling. Ethel's life, unlike Errieta's, does not provide a dramatic story. War, pandemonium, famine, and betrayal never touched her, but her life, and particularly the final third of it, was suffused with a high spiritual intensity so fine that to me it possessed a drama all its own, one of infinite tenderness and grace, and offered elements of a rare story. I'm not a bit sure I can tell it—surely not as it deserves —because it is all in delicacy of insight and intuition, composed of impressionistic, momentary glimpses, the fleeting surmise, a kaleidoscopic variety of inference. However, I want to try. Ethel was a woman whose friendship transformed the world for me. A thousand deft nuances of intelligence, wisdom, and humor made up a human magic that was inimitable, and which I would like to preserve from oblivion if I can. She would not care, but I do.

Her meadow was her private joy. Not only private, I think, but secret. During the many, many times she led me through it, pointing out a particular black-eyed Susan or a single perfect blade of grass, I don't believe I ever thought she was revealing what the meadow really meant to her, and yet I felt certain that she knew. It was, of course, an anomaly in suburban Englewood and deemed a whimsical eccentricity by most of her friends, who preferred gardens, black tulips, peonies, and delphiniums. Hid-

---

* See chapter 4 of my *Six Exceptional Women* (New York: Farrar, Straus and Giroux, 1994).

den from the street or from any neighboring viewpoint and divided in two by the split-rail fence, the nearer section of Ethel's yard was a swath of neatly clipped and flowerless lawn. The fence, with an open passage in its center, established the frontier between lawn and meadow. Beyond it the grass grew wild and high, interspersed with daisy, Queen Anne's lace, Indian paintbrush, and a narrow, sinuous path, invisible from beyond the fence, led down and around, in and out of this meadow. It was wide and deep, home to a variety of small animals, insects, the occasional garter snake. Seated in her armchair by the window, Ethel would gaze out at her meadow meditatively and sometimes murmur, "A preserve. That's what I was looking for. Some of the wildflowers were difficult to persuade. The buttercups, for instance, were not very interested in my idea. But they grew willing in the end." And when she suggested a walk in the meadow, it always seemed an invitation to enjoy the ineffable fulfillment of the earthly paradise. But that was not all. She never spoke of it, and yet I felt certain that immortality was for her a reality as self-evident as the wildflowers she had persuaded to agree with her idea.

As I've said, things with Ethel were impressionistic. They came little by little, as they do with everyone, but with her via much more subtle byways.

Dan Platt was the ever present pole toward which her compass always pointed. I never saw him, of course, or even a photograph of him, but I assume he must have been handsome. Like most of the young men of his class and era in that part of the world, he went to Princeton, graduating magna cum laude in 1895. All his life he remained a faithful alumnus, and Princeton ultimately profited very nicely. It must have been while there, or shortly afterwards, that the collecting bug bit him, and the resulting passion was lifelong. Not many lives, indeed, are affected so completely or to such an admirable degree. In his early twenties he considered the vast variety of collecting possibilities and made a shrewd, sensible, definitive decision. Italian art was what he wanted. The French school possessed its own excellence but was already expensive and for the young Mr. Platt did not offer the spiritual resources immanent in Italian art. He was rich but not immensely wealthy, no competitor to Morgan, Mellon, or Mrs. Gardner. He would never be a client of the redoubtable Duveen. So he made a choice. Pictures by Titian, Botticelli, Fra Angelico, and Mantegna, not to mention Piero and Raphael, were beyond his means; he decided to concentrate on works he could afford but which were as yet little sought after by others, and he was particularly drawn to artists of the Sienese school, of whom the most notable were Sassetta, Giovanni di Paolo, and Lorenzo Vecchietta. In addition, he bought many works by lesser, even anonymous masters, plus the occasional Venetian painting attributed to Giovanni Bellini, or the portrait of the handsome youth by Francesco Bonsignori, as well as a quantity of pictures of Roman or Bolognese origin acquired simply for pleasure. In toto, the collection finally numbered some two hundred and fifty paintings, almost all of them bought before the First World War, and more than a thousand drawings bought afterwards, when paintings had become too expensive. All of these were crowded into the house on Booth Avenue, along with Egyptian, Greek, Etruscan, and Roman objects, fine pieces of early Italian furniture, and rare Persian carpets. Ethel participated in her husband's passion to the extent of admiring what he admired, because she admired him, and experiencing sincere excitement when he grew excited over a new acquisition, because she loved him. His collection was his life, and his wife made herself the bond which gave grace and vitality to both and, incidentally, provided for a signally happy marriage. There were, however, no children. She lamented it but never explained the reason. I might hazard a guess, but anyone can do that. Dan was always busy with his collection and the concerns that went with it. He subscribed to every publication about art that appeared in the

Western world. From these hillocks of books and magazines he cut out every photograph, glued it onto a filing card, adding his own written commentary, and gradually accumulated a highly important archive of cross-referenced photographs. Often after dinner parties, or even when alone with Ethel, he would slip away to the library, where the snip, snip, snip of his scissors could be heard as he added yet more and more documents to the archive, which gradually became nearly as vital to him as the paintings that filled his house. Ethel sometimes mentioned with a sigh this obsessive attention to the archive, but no murmur of reproach ever came from her, and the well-being of the archive became in time, as we shall see, an obsession for her as well. Certainly, they also had a social life. But this, too, like everything else, was concentrated upon paintings.

It was at the turn of the century that Dan Fellows Platt married Ethel Bliss and began buying in earnest. The search for acquisitions took him inevitably to Florence, where he naturally became acquainted with the well-known scholar Bernard Berenson, later to become the legendary B.B. He also met and cultivated connoisseurs like Charles Loeser, whose Cézannes he admired but did not envy, and men of lesser renown like Mason Perkins, Arthur Acton, and Langton Douglas. In Englewood he had few friends, because nobody there had ever heard of Simone Martini, Ambrogio Lorenzetti, or Francesco di Giorgio. Social life for him and for Ethel was centered in New York, where they dined with J. P. Morgan, the Fricks, the Philip Lehmans, and sometimes Samuel Kress, Jules Bache, or Mr. and Mrs. Horace Havemeyer. The favored pastime during these soirées was vetting pictures of uncertain authorship or authenticity. Dan Platt, with his formidable archive and exceptional visual memory, was especially skilled in distinguishing the authentic from the fake and attributing anonymous paintings to very obscure artists. More than once, he irritated collectors and dealers by denouncing works of dubious quality, but his confidence in the right discernment of his eye brooked no contradiction. Thus, for example, he lost the friendship of headstrong Helen Frick, daughter of the iron-fisted old magnate, by insisting that a panel attributed to Piero della Francesca was a work of his school but emphatically not from the hand of the master. Such were the pleasures and the uncompromising raison d'être of a man whose commitment to the appreciation of great art was paramount. We may be excused for wondering what this exclusive commitment revealed or concealed. It was too absolute to be considered merely the delight of a cultivated gentleman. Something more profound and serious was at stake. Speculation will never tell us now what it was, but Ethel must have had her idea, though she never mentioned it to me.

In 1908 Dan Fellows Platt published a book entitled *Through Italy with Car and Camera*. It describes his travels throughout the peninsula at a time when in many villages an automobile had never before been seen and provides many interesting, amusing glimpses of the traveler's experience before today's tourists began to descend upon the country as tumultuously as the barbarians in the fifth century. But the true purpose of the book is to describe the author's highly cultivated impression of the countless works of art which he indefatigably sought out, some of which were purchased en route. His comments are presented in a graceful but dated style and are impersonal to a fault. He says, "We went here, we had a breakdown there, we saw this, we visited that," and yet he never mentions that his companion was his wife. He names their chauffeur, Signor Bertoni, but nowhere is Ethel Platt specifically mentioned, nor are her impressions, pleasures, or discomforts ever evoked. One wonders why. Mr. Berenson is frequently named. Perhaps Dan Platt felt that it would be unseemly to introduce his wife to the public in print. Both Henry James and Edith Wharton, fastidious and refined as they emphatically were, wrote similar books at approximately the same time and knew some of the same people but did not feel constrained to be as personally impersonal as Dan Platt.

Ethel sometimes spoke of these travels, remembering the dust, discomfort, frequent breakdowns, the bedbugs in remote road-side inns, the wretched food, and then her husband's thrill when they found in some forgotten chapel a fresco by Orcagna as yet unknown to Mr. Berenson. These stories were always told with humorous nostalgia, never with the least insinuation of resentment or regret. At the same time, Ethel could be caustic. For example, she never took to B.B. "An arrogant little man," she called him. "Always right but always ready to change his mind, especially, I thought, if there was some benefit of prestige or other profit involved. I detested his little court, where he was always the last person to enter the room unless there was a real royalty present."

I agreed with her about Berenson, though he wrote eloquently and his humanist convictions seemed convincing. "At least he did pretty well for Mrs. Gardner," I said. "Her Titian is arguably the greatest painting in America. And he stuck to his guns over the Allendale *Nativity*, always insisted it was early Titian, not Giorgione."

"Still, he was a nasty little man," Ethel insisted, "and had a ridiculous misconception of his appeal to women, for whom, moreover, he had little respect."

By the time I had become friendly with Ethel, I had known Harold Acton for several years, so naturally I inquired about La Pietra. "Arthur Acton was really a dealer," she said. "A trifle shady, Dan thought. And she was a tough little lady from Chicago. They overdid it a bit with the footmen in livery. I always tried to see whether there were crowns on their buttons but could never make it out. I'm sure there must have been, though." She laughed without malice. "All moldering in the grave now, so no matter."

Mrs. Acton, in fact, was still living, but I didn't mention it.

Ethel was not worried about death. She had seen its face at close quarters frequently by the time we became friendly. She used to go to the cemetery in Englewood where her parents were buried and stand there beside the stream that ran through and thank them for the good life they had given her. As for her own death, she was ready. "I don't want to linger," she said, "and I've made arrangements. I have the pills in the drawer of my bedside table. When the time comes, I'll know. It's so reassuring to be ready."

When an important art collector dies, tremors of cupidity surge through the art world. Museum curators hope for bequests, dealers assess their chances of advantageous acquisitions, and collectors aspire to better their holdings by the dead man's discrimination. After Dan Platt's death from pneumonia in 1938, his widow was confronted with the problem of what to do about his collection. The archive of photographs, which by this time amounted to a staggering four hundred thousand, he bequeathed to Princeton. Ethel was heir to everything else. How to manage this inheritance was not a simple matter, because the Platt fortune had been mostly spent on buying pictures, little cash remained, and there were inheritance taxes to be paid. I once asked Ethel why she had sold a particularly beautiful Pontormo, and she replied, "Because I had to, you silly boy." Besides, I don't think she would have wanted to keep everything, much as she revered the memory and passion of Dan Platt. All in all, and everything considered, she did very creditably by the collection. Curators, dealers, and collectors all got their due and more or less what they wanted, and this from a lady of impeccable refinement who had had no experience whatsoever of the devious trickeries of the marketplace. Princeton University had a small museum—no rival to those of Yale and Harvard—and Dan Platt as an enthusiastic alumnus had given a few paintings during his lifetime. After his death, Ethel gave twenty-five more, some as gifts outright, others on indefinite loan.

The dealers lost no time in presenting their kind offices. The most assiduous and successful were a pair of brothers named E. and A. Silberman. I always thought them obsequious and slippery, though they were friends of Eleanor Roosevelt, no mean judge of character. It was she who directed them toward Ethel, with whom she had a passing acquaintance. At all events, the Silberman brothers in a few years bought forty-seven paintings from Mrs. Platt, including one of the finest, a large Sassetta of the Virgin. Georges Wildenstein, ever alert to the doings of his competitors, bought eight, one of these an exquisite Pontormo portrait of a young man. Among the collectors, Robert Lehman was first in line, but his niggardly haggling offended Ethel's sense of fair play and she sent him packing, empty-handed. She much preferred dealing with the courtly, elderly Samuel Kress, who bought twenty-two of Dan Platt's pictures, among them the four remaining Sassettas, and the finest of these eventually found their home at the National Gallery in Washington, D.C., much to Ethel's pleasure.

Then there was the business of the collection of drawings, which numbered more than sixteen hundred. Of these the finest were the Italian drawings of indisputable attribution. They numbered three hundred and eighty-eight: two by Jacobo Bassano, seventy by Luca Cambiaso, two by Caravaggio, fifty-seven by Guardi, seventy-two by Guercino, twelve by Pietro Longhi, three by Parmigianino, seven by Sebastiano Ricci, sixty-one by Salvator Rosa, ninety-one by G. B. Tiepolo, and eleven by his son, Giovanni Domenico. In addition, there were numerous sheets by artists as diverse as Gauguin, Blake, Degas, Steinlen, Rodin, Augustus John, Fuseli, Constable, Corot, and a great quantity of others. Such a resplendent trove makes one gasp with wonder and longing today. Fifty-five years ago it elicited barely a sigh, and it was essentially a sigh of indifference. Collectors of drawings were rare in Europe, virtually unheard of in America. True, there were marvelous things at the Uffizi, in the Louvre and the British Museum, at Windsor and Chatsworth, but they had been swept up long before by far-seeing eyes. In New York in the forties a Leonardo or a Raphael might make a tiny dent

in the general indifference, but at auction there was little com-
petition and prices were low. What the collecting public wanted
were sunflowers by van Gogh and porcelain nudes by Renoir.
Nobody cared two straws about Cambiaso, Guercino, or Tiepolo. Ethel didn't know what to do about all those drawings,
which would occupy an undue amount of space in the new
home she was already planning for herself. On Lexington Avenue around Sixty-third Street there was a shop specializing in
art books, with a small gallery on the first floor, run by a spare,
gray man named E. Weyhe. Dan Platt had bought many books
there. Ethel turned to Mr. Weyhe. He reluctantly agreed for old
times' sake to accept on consignment a few boxes of the best
Italian drawings at very modest prices. The finest sheets by
G. B. Tiepolo, for example, were priced at twenty-five dollars.
Not much was sold. The demand for slick etchings by medioc-
rities like Luigi Lucioni and Gerald Brockhurst was what kept
the gallery going. These were easy to sell for two or three times
the price of a Tiepolo or Guercino. After a few discouraging
years Mr. Weyhe apologetically returned the boxes, nearly intact,
to Englewood. Weary and disenchanted, Ethel gave everything
to Princeton, saving only for herself the mouse by Salvator Rosa,
a Blake, a Modigliani, two Romneys of Lady Hamilton, a wa-
tercolor by Ruskin, and a drawing by Burne-Jones. And that's
how the collection of drawings at Princeton University became
overnight one of the most important in America.

Ah, Princeton. When Dan Platt went there, long before the
flippant days of Scott Fitzgerald and Bunny Wilson, it must,
indeed, have been a sort of paradise for the rich, well-bred,
good-looking lads like him. He kept faith with the memory all
his life, and his wife, whose parents had never dreamed of send-
ing her to college, participated with emotion in his golden nostalgia. It was golden for Princeton, anyway. She loved to drive
down there, especially in the spring, when the magnolias were
in bloom, stroll about the campus, have lunch at the Inn, then

drive back to Englewood. The Princeton magnolias, she maintained, were the most beautiful in all the world. Often, if I was
in America at the time, she asked me to drive her down there,
and I was happy to do so, though I never cared for the place.
All three of my brothers had gone there, though not I, being
too stupid, and I counted the exclusion a blessing. We went to
the museum, housed then in an old, nondescript building, and
Ethel pointed out to me many of the paintings that had belonged to her husband. Not all were hanging, and not a single
drawing. The most important and imposing, though small, was
a panel by Giovanni di Paolo representing the Madonna with
Saints Margaret and Catherine of Alexandria. It was beautiful
and rare, considered by connoisseurs to be one of the master's
most accomplished and spiritual works. Dan Platt had particularly prized it, and that was why Ethel had never sold it despite
the pleading of the Silberman brothers, and had deposited it at
Princeton only on indefinite loan. Belonging still to her, she felt,
it still belonged to him. The director of the museum was a wispy,
affable man named Ernest De Wald, who greeted Ethel with
deference. She asked to see her husband's archive of photographs. De Wald was hesitant and apologetic, explaining that for
lack of funds and adequate personnel it had not proved possible
to tend to the archive as conscientiously as it deserved. But he
took us down to the basement nonetheless to see it. The spectacle was a shock. All those hundreds of thousands of photographs meticulously catalogued, mounted on filing cards, and
held in fabric bindings were now falling to pieces. Ancient glue
had dried, photographs become torn and detached from filing
cards and replaced any which way, some of them left on the
floor where they had fallen, the whole archive housed on sagging
metal shelves, powdered with dust and obviously left to deteri-
orate in indifference and neglect. Ethel picked up the photographs that lay on the floor and very gently placed them on top
of a few others. She said not a word. De Wald apologized again

and tactlessly remarked that the photograph collection in the Frick Art Reference Library, available to students, was, in any case, far more complete and profited from a large endowment. Ethel nodded in wordless agreement. Then we took our leave amid an exemplary show of good manners by all. Driving back to Englewood, Ethel said, "Dan Platt devoted his whole life to creating that archive. Miss Frick got the idea from him. His whole life. And to see it now in that cellar. It was like going to his funeral for the second time."

Not knowing what to say, I knew enough to say nothing. Ethel never again mentioned the archive in my presence, and I think I was the only one with whom she had seen its ruin. We sometimes went to Princeton after that but visited the museum again only once.

She did not care for Schopenhauer and considered the desert of his personal life to be evidence ipso facto that his philosophy of pessimism was intellectually and morally sterile. Conversations with her could take unexpected, tortuous, and demanding turns. I knew next to nothing about formal philosophical discourse, but she had read widely and deeply, and was a friend of Hannah Arendt, with whom she had abstruse conversations. Ethel preferred Kant, whose tolerant humanism she praised, often citing as an ideal ethic the categorical imperative which maintains that one must act as if the principle from which one acts were to become through one's will a universal law. I wondered whether general application of this proposition might not in practice have catastrophic consequences, and I fear it has. But I enjoyed talking with Ethel about ideas. She would hold her forefinger against her temple, incline her head slightly to the right, gaze out at her meadow, and muse upon the supreme themes of human thought. I've never talked with anyone else as I did with her, because with her what was most complex seemed intelligible by reason of her intellectual and emotional identification with what is metaphysical, therefore essential to the good life. Frequently, I didn't know what I was talking about, but that didn't seem to matter, as if a legitimate part of philosophy were precisely to talk about matters that eluded one's understanding. Socrates, who understood nearly everything, certainly would have said so.

Our conversations in the afternoon were by no means limited to topics of high seriousness. Ethel loved a good laugh, even a joke in relatively poor taste. She was not interested in politics except on the elevated, theoretical plane familiar to Hannah Arendt. But we joked about political figures and wondered how in the world entire populations could believe them to be real people. Hitler was no joke, certainly, nor was Stalin, but viewed from the perspective of a Kafka, even they could be seen as ghastly, ghoulish, Black Death buffoons. And Ethel's laughter really was the music of the spheres, so delicate and rippling on the surface of her throat like a song—*An die Musik*—lighted by a slightly melancholy gleam in the gray eyes. We had fun with each other, in short. Of course, there was plenty of talk about the Masaccios in the Church of the Carmine in Florence, the Benozzo Gozzolis in the Palazzo Medici-Riccardi, the Pinturicchios in Siena, and the Signorellis in Orvieto—the Masaccios being infinitely the best, needless to add; Dan Platt had always said so.

After two or three years I came and went at 200 Cedar Street almost as simply as if it were my right, having only to telephone a quarter of an hour before in order to be sure I'd be welcome. Ethel had a few other friends, but not many. There could be something intimidating about her queenly intellectual manner, although at the same time she was utterly unaffected and perfectly prepared, for example, to discuss the proper raising of poultry. In fact, she would have liked to have a few chickens in her meadow, though not a very practical proposition in suburban Englewood with its many dogs.

My friendship with Mrs. Platt surprised my parents, so I de-

cided to bring them together, and in order to make the first
meeting more easily congenial I asked Ethel's friends the Atchleys to join us. The occasion, a cocktail party at my parents'
house, was jolly, but I was surprised to observe my mother,
whom I would have expected to have much in common with
Ethel, shy and reserved, whereas my father, who certainly had
less familiarity than his wife with intellectual and aesthetic concerns, hit it off at once in a spirit of old school conviviality with
his guest. In time, my mother became warmer and more at ease.
Maybe she sensed that I shared with Ethel, as I did, a relation
of refinement and intellectual compatibility in which she was not
initially invited to participate. She knew, however, and never
doubted that no other attachment could ever match my filial
devotion to her. In time, the three of us spent many happy
moments together. We went to the Metropolitan Museum and
had lunch afterwards in the Hotel Stanhope's bland dining
room. We went to the Cloisters and the Museum of Modern
Art, but never to the Frick. Too many memories there, I assumed. My father rarely accompanied us on these outings, but
when we went to Cedar Street for drinks Ethel always said,
"Albert, you must mix the cocktails, please. Nobody else has
your way with the shaker." I was glad that my parents became
Ethel's friends, because she had few, and in the end my mother
and father offered her more comfort and kept her more company than anyone else. She had no close relatives of her own,
having been an only child, and Dan Platt's cousins saw her
seldom.

In 1955 I took an apartment in New York. When I mentioned
to Ethel that I had no furniture, she said that a lot of fine pieces
from the house on Booth Avenue were still in storage and I
could borrow all I wanted. So my one-room studio was furnished with things that would have looked all right in the Pitti
Palace. But I only stayed there for a year. The lure of Paris was
too potent to be denied. When I was abroad, we corresponded.

Ethel's letters were like her. I choose only a single one, but it is similar to many and many another.

200 Cedar Street
Englewood, New Jersey
June 10th, 1957

Dear Jim,

I am happy to learn that you are comfortably back in Paris and have recovered from the mumps. That ridiculous ailment can be rather a nuisance for adults. I hope it wasn't too fearfully painful. The girl with whom I cut out paper dolls as a child came down with a severe case and I was put in quarantine as a result. But I never developed the malady and enjoyed quarantine so much that I told my father I wanted to remain in quarantine for the rest of my life. Perhaps I have. What do you think? Isolation has never been forced upon me, but I have derived much pleasure from it. There is such a multitude of good company just outside my window. You remember the magic painting of St. Francis by Bellini [in the Frick Collection] and all the creatures that were his companions. I have no donkey but as for the rest am reasonably well provided for.

Last week I went to the club for luncheon with your mother and Mary Atchley. The headwaiter always calls your mother Lady Lord and me Lady Platt but Mary is only Mrs. Atchley, which irritates her so considerably that she orders a second frozen daiquiri and smokes two or three extra cigarettes. Mary has not yet recovered from being the smartest girl at the University of Chicago and she's now well past eighty.

Lately I have been dipping into Proust more or less at random. We all know the parts to skip. At the same time I have looked a little more carefully into Bergson, who is said to have had an important influence on P. Indeed he did! Why is it that works of imagination so often receive more praise than works of thought? Bergson maintained that only by intuition can one grasp the reality of time, which is duration applied to the life experience, and the incidence of memory is the verification of duration. Does this by any chance remind you of the relation between external and internal reality to be discovered in time and memory? I think I'd admire P. more if he'd been a little less intelligent. But the wonderful characters remain eternally wonderful. The poor old baron is my favorite. I really can't go along, though, with the notion that artistic creation is superior to nature.

The meadow, by the way, is doing very nicely under hot afternoon sunshine. We have buttercups and daisies already and there are signs of exciting buds to bloom before the season of goldenrod. Bobolinks have come and gone, blue jays are eternal and I've got my eye on a red-headed woodpecker that is considering my sycamore. Won't you come and watch it make up its mind? I'd be ever so pleased if you did.

Fond regards,

Ethel

Whether the woodpecker decided to make its home in her sycamore I never knew, but I'm sure she did. I didn't return to Englewood until early November. The meadow then was nearly finished, but we took our ritual stroll down and around the circuitous path and saw the leftovers of summer's glory. It had never been more true to itself, she said, adding that some people in Englewood considered her a little tetched because she went to so much trouble for a very ordinary field. "Obviously," she remarked, "they would have considered William Blake deranged."

Of all the people I have known—and I've known several renowned gardeners—Ethel, I think, had the closest intimacy with nature. Errieta was very close, but she let nature come to her, as it were, rather than releasing herself, as Ethel did, entirely to its mysteries and marvels. She believed in something that surpassed the human capacity for intelligible belief, not something she would have called God or any other divinity with some resemblance to humankind, but something numinous, pantheistic, transcendental, in which one could merge one's identity for the sake of a kind of supernatural ecstasy that became the true incarnation of nature. She had long lived among works of art, some of them masterpieces, but I believe she'd have surrendered them all for one dandelion. And eventually that is more or less what she did.

There is a national park called Bear Mountain up the Hudson

River beyond Nyack. In October on a fine day she liked to take a picnic lunch and drive up there in her antiquated car, an Oldsmobile about twenty years old in immaculate condition which had only a very few thousand miles on its speedometer. There was a high outcropping of sunburnt rock in a lonely corner of the park, a spot she'd discovered where other visitors never intruded. I sometimes went with her on these outings, of which the purpose was to admire the crimson, golden blaze of autumnal foliage. She knew her way up the steep incline and clambered to the top with daring agility, indifferent to the fact that a fall at her age could be calamitous. And there we would perch on the highest boulder, our picnic spread before us, eating deviled eggs, smoked-salmon sandwiches, figs and dates, and drinking cold water from a thermos jug which Dan Platt had perennially pampered on the travels throughout Italy. We spoke very little while enthroned up there amid the heartbreaking outburst of beauty before seasonal decease. The first time I'd gone to Bear Mountain with Ethel, I had made the mistake of imagining that speech might magnify what eyes could barely fathom, so I said something superficial about the splendor of the sight surrounding us. "Don't talk," she said gently. "Let the leaves compose their own hymn." No more intimation was needed. Our visits thereafter to Bear Mountain in the autumn partook of something reverential.

Going to Princeton to admire the magnolias was not at all the same. It was joyful, talkative, exhilarating. Ethel went almost yearly to Princeton in the spring, but Princeton, I noticed, never came to Englewood. Nor did Princeton, for that matter, ever entreat Ethel to visit Princeton. Not once did any official from the university invite himself to Cedar Street to make a seemly gesture of recognition for all that the old lady who lived there, not to mention her husband, had done to glorify the Princeton Museum of Art. The neglect was probably not deliberate, which to my mind only made it worse. Perhaps Princeton felt that the Platts had given so much that nothing worth having remained to be given and therefore an aged donor could politely be left to die without so much as an annual Christmas card to commemorate past munificence. What Ethel thought of this egregious indifference I had no idea and knew better than to mention it. I was delighted, however, to discover one day how dearly a great university can pay for being neglectful.

She called me one Wednesday evening early in 1960, when I was in Englewood visiting my parents, and asked whether I would escort her down to Princeton the following Saturday. She had an errand to take care of there and did not want to go alone. I was happy to agree. To drive from Englewood to Princeton takes little more than an hour at reasonable speed. The day was a gray one early in March, the fifth. Ethel, often talkative and sprightly, was uncommonly quiet that afternoon, almost glum, which puzzled me, as it was unlike her to allow her mood to be perceptible behind her good manners. I did not try to make conversation. To intrude upon Ethel's unspoken thoughts was unthinkable.

When we reached Princeton, she said, "Please take me to the museum." Once there, she asked a receptionist for Mr. De Wald, replying to the girl's inquiry, "I am Mrs. Dan Fellows Platt."

The director promptly appeared, and after a smiling shake of hands with us both, rubbed his own together jovially, as if he expected Ethel to produce a few more Tiepolos and a Guardi or two. Instead, she tersely said, "I've come to take back the Giovanni di Paolo."

"Oh no," cried Mr. De Wald. "It's the finest thing we have."

"It happens to be the finest thing *I* have," said Ethel. "I left it here on loan only, and I want it now, this afternoon."

"Of course, of course," murmured the dejected De Wald. We followed him into the central gallery of the museum, where the Giovanni di Paolo hung in a place of honor, framed and under glass. De Wald lifted the heavy frame from the wall and placed it in my hands, turning to Ethel as he did so, saying, "Are you absolutely sure? Such a loss to Princeton. What would Mr. Platt say?"

"Mr. Platt," Ethel replied with some hauteur, "would say that Mrs. Platt is now alone to speak for the hereafter, and so I have. Jim, if you will put the picture in the trunk, we can be on our way." I gently placed the fifteenth-century masterpiece in the trunk of the Oldsmobile. Then we shook hands with the despondent Mr. De Wald and drove away.

Ethel was more talkative during the ride back to Englewood, but neither then nor later did she ever hint at her reasons for having taken away from Princeton an artistic treasure which they could never replace. I thought I knew why she'd done it, but I also knew that with Ethel it was unrealistic to assume that one ever understood what thoughts or feelings were the keys or formulas of action. If questioned, I had long since realized, she was quite capable of responding:

> After the torchlight red on sweaty faces
> After the frosty silence in the gardens
> After the agony in stony places
> The shouting and the crying
> He who was living is now dead
> We who were living are now dying.

It was not for nothing that Ethel had lived for so long with the products of mythology and mysticism or that poetry sprang spontaneously from her memory when the answer to a question was itself the question. When we came back to Cedar Street, we hung the Giovanni di Paolo in the living room on a side wall adjacent to the large contemporary altarpiece by Taddeo di Bartolo. It was not to remain there for very long.

Her birthday was October 25. In 1962 on that date, a decade after our first meeting, I went out to Englewood to see her, taking a bouquet. We had lunch alone together at the table by the far window. Afterwards, while sipping our coffee from Dresden cups, we sat on either side of the low Italian table, and Ethel said, "You remember the scene in *Der Rosenkavalier* when the Marschallin looks into the mirror and says, 'It's time.' She was only about thirty-five, of course. I'm considerably more than twice that and I don't need a mirror to know that it's time to start getting ready. I don't want to leave a lot of flotsam behind. I'd like you to have a souvenir of Cedar Street, something that Dan Platt set store by, and I thought of the Blake drawing. If that would give you pleasure."

"The very greatest, as you know," I said.

"Good," said Ethel with her timeless smile. "Then that's settled."

It was a drawing of extraordinary finesse, the study for an illustration to *Night Thoughts* by Edward Young, a nude male blowing a long trumpet held between his outstretched hands. I didn't try to express thanks but kissed her as I left, hung the drawing beside my bed, and wrote her a long letter, of which she never made mention.

E. and A. Silberman were both dead, Mr. Kress likewise, and Georges Wildenstein had been replaced by his disagreeable son Daniel. Ethel was no longer in touch with anyone familiar to her in the New York art world. I, on the other hand, thanks largely to my efforts to raise money for the purchase of Cézanne's studio in Aix-en-Provence, knew a good many people, and Ethel, who had contributed generously for Cézanne, was aware of it. Consequently, I was not too startled when she called to tell me that she was resolved to continue with the program of eliminating from among her possessions what she felt to be inessential and had decided to dispose first of the Giovanni di Paolo because it was the most valuable thing she owned. She didn't need the money, but of all things to leave behind, money was likely to be most convenient and least trouble. Could I assist her in negotiating the sale? It was easy, as I knew just the dealer in New York prepared to pay well for an Old Master of prestigious provenance and iron-clad authenticity. He was, in fact, a friend, and still is; his wife, moreover, was someone I have known since childhood. Negotiations were necessary in order to establish the price, but Ethel was no skinflint and the dealer was prepared to pay well for something which a lifetime of waiting might never provide again. The Giovanni di Paolo eventually went, I believe, to a museum in Texas, where that magisterial depiction of Quattrocento piety must be somewhat lonely.

The rest of the paintings and drawings did not have to wait long to follow the Giovanni di Paolo away from Cedar Street. The same dealer who had bought the first painting bought the rest, and it was he who gave me the Bonsignori portrait of the handsome Venetian youth as a gratuity for having arranged the sales. For her part, Ethel insisted on giving me the Tiepolo head of a woman and the two drawings by Romney. I protested, but she was adamant, and said that Dan Platt had always been a stickler for giving commissions even to friends like Mason Perkins when they found a picture for him. "And you'll be helping me to make a clean sweep," she added. These departures made for a lot of empty wall space in Ethel's house, for only the Luini angel, the mouse by Salvator Rosa, and the Burne-Jones drawing of a Pre-Raphaelite maiden now remained. The angel was promised as a legacy to a relative of Dan Platt. As for the mouse and the maiden, where they went I never knew. It did not prove difficult to fill the empty spaces, because Ethel had in her attic a stock of framed reproductions which Dan Platt had bought for documentary purposes. Together we hung these wherever the vanished paintings had been, and though the house would never again be as pure and rare, it satisfied its inhabitant. "What a relief at last to be done with all that," she exclaimed. "Dan once said to me, 'Effie, I've given more of my life to my collection and my archive than I should have done. I couldn't help myself, but I don't want you to do the same.' And I haven't. The furniture will simply have to take care of itself."

Wearying of the ugliness and violence of New York, I had moved to a beautiful house on a hilltop in Old Lyme, Connecticut, but I went back regularly to Englewood to visit my parents and never missed an opportunity to call at Cedar Street. Ethel was growing old, but when the weather was fine we still followed the serpentine path through the meadow, and I marveled at the freshness of her excitement when she spied an unexpected flower or out-of-season butterfly. The spontaneous delight of the girl who had driven her pony cart under the mulberry trees was still hers, such a wonder to behold that, indeed, no work of art could compare with it. Sometimes my emotion was almost stronger than my ability to contain it. I had come to her in the beginning with the intent to admire. That I did. In the end it was love that led me on, but I never could say so. Probably she knew. Her intuition was one of the marvels of her friendship.

I hadn't forgotten her having said that she didn't want to linger and that when the time came she'd know what to do with the pills in the drawer of her bedside table. I believed her. She always expressed herself with the forthright sincerity of someone who has not been afraid of life's dark corners. That's how she was able to see a world in a grain of sand and a heaven in a wildflower—like Blake, she said—hold infinity in the palm of her hand and eternity in an hour.

The time did come, of course, as it does for everyone and everything, but by then the clock of certainty was no longer accurate. It was an early evening of exceptional warmth in the late autumn of 1970. Sitting in her chair by the window, Ethel saw a firefly in the meadow. Astonished at this unseasonable apparition, she rose to go outside and have a closer look at the phenomenal bug. Just outside the front door, she fell full length onto the ground. Whether she had tripped over one of the paving stones of her front walk and been stunned by the fall or had momentarily lost consciousness and consequently fallen was never clear. When after a few moments she came to herself and called for the faithful Netty, luckily her voice carried well, and the maid helped her to her room, put her to bed, and telephoned Ethel's doctor. Examination disclosed that, whatever the cause, she had suffered a slight stroke. She would not be gravely incapacitated, but would never again be quite herself. The inevitable recourse was the nursing home, where she would find no bedside table with the desirable pills in its drawer.

It was a very comfortable, even luxurious place that went by the ludicrous, lugubrious name of Dunrovin. I went there to see Ethel on several occasions with my parents, who were by that time almost the only regular visitors she had. Her room was pleasant. The Burne-Jones drawing hung on the wall facing the bed in which she lay, attired in various elegant crêpe-de-chine bed jackets. Sometimes she was perfectly lucid, sometimes incomprehensibly vague, but it was never clear that she knew exactly where she was. Her meadow, in any case, remained very distinct in her mind and memory. One could almost believe— or believe that she believed—that it lay just beyond her window, as it had on Cedar Street. The last time I saw her was on February 28, 1971, a Sunday. My parents and I tried to make conversation, but it didn't go easily. She kept saying to my father, "Albert, please fetch the cocktail shaker. We'll all have a cocktail to celebrate." But even Dunrovin was not luxurious enough to allow for cocktail parties. After a time we prepared to leave and said goodbye. Ethel glanced at us with apparent surprise and said, "How kind of you to invite me. Someday you must visit my home. If the weather is fine, we can walk in the meadow. Now, don't forget. My name is Effie Bliss." And then she smiled serenely, the radiant smile of her almost endless youth.

It was four months and some days later that she died, having outlived Dan Platt by more than three decades. Her remains were interred in the selfsame cemetery where she had so often gone to thank the dead for her miraculous life.

Envoi

Writers' lives by and large are not very interesting. To spend a lifetime seated at a desk searching for the *mot juste* is a monotonous, self-indulgent, virtually maniacal business. One thinks, of course, that there are exceptions: the giant literary geniuses—Tolstoy, Henry James, Joyce, Proust—whose great creations have generated great curiosity about their lives and have provided the raw material for biographical works almost equal in conceptual power to their own. Even these men, however, did not lead happy, enviable lives, sustained by the rightful satisfactions of professional fulfillment. But they *were* interesting, because their objective was to create the life beyond life evoked with such feeling by Milton, the blind poet who, like Homer, peered so deeply into the human predicament.

From the time of my early adolescence, I never ceased yearning to become a writer. Writing, I thought, would let me soar above the mundane throng, mastery of words providing the wings. Had I known then what mastery is needed in order to soar, words alone providing next to no levitation, I would have made a different deal with the devil. But the sacred alibi of youth is the purity of ignorance. I read the biographies of men who had truly soared and had paid the Icarus price for it. I learned nothing. Noticing, though, that eminent men had frequently been acquainted with men of eminence, I fancied that that rule might somehow one day do something for me. Then the Second World War graciously furnished an opportunity by taking me to Paris, where I hastened to ring Picasso's doorbell. He welcomed me with courtesy and curiosity. When in order to possess tangible verification of the prestige of his acquaintance I asked him to draw my portrait, he did it. Unsatisfied by this first likeness, I asked him later to draw another, and he did it again. So I naïvely assumed that I'd set one foot across the threshold of posterity's mansion, little dreaming I had neither the wit nor the courage to dwell in solitary confinement. And of course I wrote down in my diary all that had happened and been said. But I had no agenda. What drew out the words was merely the magnet of self-importance.

Intrepid indeed must be the pathfinder who ventures upon the perilous route of the diarist. It is dangerous because it invites the inventor to invent himself, to plead for sympathy when none is due, to seek inadmissible esteem, and to pine for illicit advantage in love. This being so commonplace a risk—the issue of literary skill left charitably in limbo—the very best thing that most authors of diaries can do is to burn them. Failing that, a diarist with any sense will write very sparingly about himself. Unless he is a commentator of Boswellian stature—and even Boswell realized that someone else must deliver the ticket to posthumous renown—he will seek to make himself interesting by describing and defining, should providence have bestowed the necessary aptitude and intelligence, what it is that constitutes the interest of persons far more interesting than he is. By doing that, he gives himself a better chance of providing a meaningful self-portrait than by dwelling on the butterfly pursuits of his private life.

I began to keep a diary when I was fifteen and have made the habit lifelong. These notebooks have been useful to me, but I have been a conscientious burner, too, and when I'm gone, none will remain to indict me. On the other hand, I've been a scrupulous saver of letters, hoping at the same time, like Henry James in his innocence, that all of my own will have perished. Some of my letters which may unfortunately have survived were written to Thomas Mann, the author I most admired when young, whom I admire still, in fact. He was dutifully responsive to appeals from the young. Though we never met, we had a correspondence lasting over a number of years, and in a letter written on December 13, 1947, he said, "You seem to possess the attributes which above all enable a talented person to learn. I mean the gift for admiration. It is this gift to which my own artistic growth owes most."

Mann was right. I have continually hoped to meet men and women I could truly admire. Admiration that transfigures one's view of experience involves a disposition toward the romantic. One must believe in miracles, which are simply instances of inexplicable revelation: the blind see visions of perfection, the deaf hear the music of the spheres. These things do happen. They are beyond the reach of reason, and that is their power to transform a life. I know, having lived for the enrichment of such accidents. They don't occur because you want them to but because childhood is always in search of amazement. And I have been lucky, having bumped into an extraordinary number of remarkable people, many of whom I admired. This happens when the meanders of the creative itinerary lead across a couple of real and imaginary continents and when you have enough money and determination to travel by the footpath rather than the main highway. And take along no maps.

It was thirty years ago on a farm in Connecticut that I first thought it might someday be worth my while to write a few memoirs. Even then, I'd already known a lot of interesting people, some of them admirable, and imagined I might do worse than try to make their interest and my admiration work together for the benefit of a more general admiration and interest. So I set aside the mediocre novel I was laboring over and wrote with pleasure and relative ease a piece called *Where the Pictures Were*, an account of my acquaintance with Gertrude Stein and Alice B. Toklas. That first effort was an experiment, and it turned out to seem relatively successful. Consequently, I resolved to try my hand at others later on. A long, long time intervened before I got around to trying, mainly because I devoted fifteen exhilarating, arduous years to preparing the biography of Alberto Giacometti. When that job was done, however, I remembered the pleasure I'd enjoyed while writing about Gertrude and Alice and thought I had nothing better to do than attempt other experiments of the same genre.

A memoir is a narrative of indeterminate length composed from personal experience and is presumed to be the record of something noteworthy. It is inevitably, then, written in the first person but is not strictly speaking supposed to be an account of the writer's own life. Autobiography proper implies self-creation as well as self-criticism, and as such is essentially a post-Romantic form despite the remarkable *Meditations* of Marcus Aurelius and *Confessions* of Saint Augustine. Heralded by Rousseau's own self-serving Confessions, the modern era has brought forth a few outstanding autobiographies by such men as T. E. Lawrence and Robert Graves. But they, of course, had genuine adventures to relate, had lived lives of compelling interest, and were redoubtable masters of language. On no score could I ever have expected to be of their company. Nor did I aspire to. I have seen greatness at close enough range to realize that I do not possess the bravery, the ingenuity, or the pertinacity to endure the travail involved. I have led an exceptionally fortunate and pleasant life. At age seventy-five I have never been seriously ill, either physically or mentally, and since my release from the U.S. Army in 1945 have been able to do exactly as I pleased, though misguided through a couple of decades of laborious apprenticeship as to the dynamics of enlightened pleasure. I have been lucky in love and friendship. The evidence is conclusive. An account of my life would not be very interesting, would it? Still, my luck in friendship made me acquainted with quite a lot of interesting, exceptional, remarkable, and admirable men and women, and it was by writing about them that I thought to try to create a ripple of interest among people who would understandably never have been interested in me.

An Envoi is usually the concluding, explanatory passage of a poem, essay, or book. In this case there are four books, but all of them in my mind have from the beginning formed a single entity united by my desire to know and frequent and write about people whom I have liked or, even better—mindful of Thomas Mann's assumption—admired. I truly believe there has been something to admire in those I have chosen to commemorate. Each was in his, or her, own manner committed to a spiritual, moral, or intellectual ideal that does make a person's experience unusual and, indeed, admirable. Friendship, as I say, has been the cement of my memoirs, but now that the building is complete, now that I can view it from a distance, see it in the round, and consider what sort of structure it stands for, so to speak, an intuition seems to tell me that I have produced an edifice more suggestive than I bargained for. It begins to look like the memorial to a vanished world. All the individuals I have endeavored to lure into my life from the tip of my pen shared a sense of the indispensable relation between creativity and daily experience. Artists, writers, composers, ladies of the beau monde or the demi, couturiers, men of fashion and of turpitude, rich and poor, straight and gay, they were united in a social homogeneity that acknowledged and personified the vivifying significance of art. I was lucky enough to be able to observe at first hand many, many scenes illustrative of this very diverse unity. Only with wistful, unrealistic yearning can one evoke them today, those fragments built into the architecture of my memories like the bits and pieces of classical sculpture long ago used as material to raise the walls of a now abandoned fortress along the shore of the Bosphorus. Approximately a score of such fragments are set into my books. Glimpses, recollections of them come to me now as I write. They come to me often at other times as well. Only last night, for example, I dreamed of Balthus. And today I think with deep sadness of Dora, having just this morning learned of her death. Maybe some images of these fragments will adumbrate a theme which, perhaps, is the basic idea that unbeknownst to me provided the foundation upon which I rashly built.

In Picasso's studio I see the Communist authors and zealots, Aragon and Eluard, both tall men, bending over the short painter, whispering at him conspiratorially, one into each ear, while Picasso gazed up into the air as if hoping for the salvation of some capitalistic deus ex machina, which he lavishly received but never repaid.

Gertrude Stein, while delivering herself of those celebrated monologues, liked to stand below her portrait by Picasso, which hung above the fireplace against a mirror. Repetition, she used to say, is meaning. I wasn't sure what to make of this pronouncement. Is a rose thrice affirmed a rose a rose more roseate than any other? The soldiers in Miss Stein's salon would surely have said yes, and she, after all, had written that yes is for a very young man.

Alice Toklas, hunched in her horsehair fauteuil under the orange halo of lamplight in which the whorls of Pall Mall smoke drifted like galaxies, listened attentively to the latest news of Virgil

Thomson related by Thornton Wilder, who strode to and fro, cigarette also in hand. He, of course, had been present at the premiere of *Four Saints in Three Acts* in Hartford, Connecticut.

Arletty, bedridden, blind, never forgot that she owed her career to Paul Guillaume, the celebrated art dealer, whom she had met on the sidewalk. In the darkness of her final years, at four o'clock in the morning, unable to sleep, she used to sing again and again the songs that had first made her famous in the musical revues of Rip, the impresario to whom Guillaume introduced her. She said, "If I can remember the songs, I remember the men who made it possible for me to sing them, and then I won't forget who I am myself."

Goyas gazed down upon the guests in Marie-Laure de Noailles's octagonal salon. They were likely to be Man Ray, the photographer, or Francis Poulenc, the composer, or Balthus, the painter, or Yves Saint-Laurent, the couturier, or a cowboy from Camargues, or a writer like James Lord. And how we all talked and talked about the latest exhibition at the Galerie Claude Bernard, the recent novel by Nathalie Sarraute or the performance in Etienne de Beaumont's ballroom of Erik Satie's *Socrate* sung by Maria Freund, who had created it in 1918. My friends have told me that I failed to be altogether fair to a faithful friend and drew more of a caricature than an accurate portrait. There is some truth in this. But Marie-Laure was of her own volition very much of a caricature, and she would never have objected to remembrance of that aspect of her personality. She was also, however, a lady of rare cultivation and perspicacity, capable of subtle judgment and openhanded acts of kindness. No doubt, I should have emphasized more forcefully that very appealing fact of her character, for it much endeared her to her many friends.

.   .   .

In her lamplit, white-walled living room, Errieta Perdikidi carefully placed her ancient phonograph on a low table and brought
out an album of records made by the Busch Quartet in the
twenties. I was there with Christian Davillerd. Also present was
Kostas Axelos, the philosopher, with his wife, Rhea. Errieta suggested that she play one of Beethoven's last quartets, Number 13 in B-flat major. The record was worn, the machine in
poor repair. Yet here was Beethoven, magisterial, sublime, and
to sit there listening to his music on that island at the far end
of Europe seemed to imply that civilization, even when it came
to an end, when our sun was made a cinder, would not have
been for nothing, and that, without having to say so, we all
recognized Errieta to be a precious representative of it.

In the grand salon of his parents' sumptuous Florentine villa,
Harold Acton dearly loved to receive celebrated literary guests.
Few eminent authors managed to slip through the City of Lilies
without the ritual visit to La Pietra. Somerset Maugham and his
companion Alan Searle were there one day when I was present.
A few years before, I had visited Maugham at his villa on Cap-
Ferrat, been shown his art collection, and thought the pictures
all "easy" examples by Renoir, Toulouse-Lautrec, Picasso, Gauguin, Marie Laurencin, et al. On the occasion of this Florentine
meeting I was preoccupied by efforts to preserve Cézanne's studio and I thought to ask Maugham why he owned no work by
that great artist. The author replied, "I'm n-n-not intellectual
enough. All the c-c-critics will t-t-tell you so." Harold said,
"Come, come, Willie, what twaddle."

Cocteau, too, hungered for the company of distinguished creative persons. As he was prone to do all the talking, however, I

seldom saw him with any. Julien Green once came to the Villa Santo Sospir while I was there. Jean, having lately returned from a visit to Spain, had perfected one of his glittery monologues about gypsy dwarfs, El Greco's eyesight, Isabel la Católica, the interior of Saint Teresa's *Interior Castle*, bullfights, flamenco-Coca-Cola, and so on and on. Green didn't stay long. Then there was the unfortunate visit to Picasso in Vallauris, when Jean talked about old times to a fare-thee-well, about Diaghilev and Massine, Etienne de Beaumont's soirées, *Parade*, Madame Errazuriz, Picasso's marriage, at which he had been one of the witnesses, and I can't recall how much else. Maybe it was the excess of loquacity that prompted the painter to gratify his old friend with such an insulting farewell memento.

Balthus knew almost all the painters and writers of his era, even Dalí, whom he despised. But as he grew older he preferred the company of aristocrats and wealthy admirers. The only colleague with whom he always maintained an intimate friendship was Giacometti. I recall one afternoon with them at the Café de Flore when they argued at length over the perceptible dimensions of Géricault's *Raft of the Medusa* should it be viewed on the far side of the boulevard, Alberto loudly insisting that at such a distance it would appear to be only a few centimeters in height, while Balthus calmly maintained that its appearance would correspond exactly to its actual size because one saw what one knew rather than what one merely hypothesized. They never agreed, of course, but enjoyed arguing. Alberto was the better dialectician.

Giacometti knew everybody, and everybody he knew sought him out, because his company and conversation were so original, challenging, and entertaining. But Alberto enjoyed seeing his friends *en tête-à-tête*, not in groups. He never introduced me to anyone. I ran into Jean Genet at the studio one day when Alberto was absent, not a pleasant encounter. Then I saw Balthus and Alberto together several times, but that was always due to arrangements made by Balthus, not by Alberto. One afternoon Alberto and I were alone together in the café at the corner of the rue Didot and the rue d'Alésia when a journalist appeared and introduced himself to the artist. A lengthy conversation ensued between Alberto and the unknown newcomer, lasting at least thirty or forty minutes, during which not one word was addressed to me. It was as if I had ceased to be present. When the journalist finally departed, I made some protest, maintaining that it had been impolite to ignore me so completely. Alberto laughed and said that I could have joined the conversation if I'd wished to, adding, "You must understand that I'm just as interested in someone I've known for ten minutes as in someone I've known for ten years."

Henry McIlhenny cultivated the company of cultivated people. He enjoyed dining with Kenneth Clark, Yehudi Meuhin, W. H. Auden, and Greta Garbo just as much as with Princess Margaret or the Duchess of Westminster. He always had something sensible to say to each one of his guests. I remember the repasts in his dining room with a Chardin, a Cézanne, and a Matisse on one wall, as moments when one could almost believe that civilization was likely to last forever.

Sonia Orwell and Peter Watson dedicated their lives to the creative life. Their friends were writers and painters, Bacon, Lucian Freud and John Craxton, Stephen and Natasha Spender, T. S. Eliot and John Hayward, Benjamin Britten and Peter Pears, a flock of others. Sonia once said, "Talking with a poet for five minutes makes me feel richer than discussing contracts with a publisher for an hour." Peter posed for two portraits by Giacometti, who made him a gift of the finer one and always spoke of him with admiration as "a man of the world in the world of art." He was also portrayed by Lucian, who may not have guessed how greatly he was to be admired.

Isabel Rawsthorne's four husbands, her countless lovers, her host of friends all were soldiers in the war of the poetic versus the prosaic. And so was she, not the least courageous when it came to battling the bourgeois. I can hear her copper laughter still, even as the munitions of beauty and youth were nearly exhausted. The wine did *flow* in Sudbury Cottage, it's true, but when everything had been said again and again by Alan and Francis and Isabel herself, it fortified the lifelong intoxication of art.

For almost forty years in the wake of the Second World War nearly every artist, art critic, art curator, and art collector of any consequence—and many of none—who came to Venice visited Peggy Guggenheim's palazzo. She enjoyed admiration, and there was plenty about her to admire. Having amassed with little money an invaluable collection of art, she had the abiding ambition to let it be admired *in aeternum* even by people who don't believe in immortality. So I like to extol Peggy's optimistic conviction that Venice will never be vanquished by the sea.

With Ethel Platt, though our friendship was woven on the loom of aesthetic compatibility, I never met a single artist or writer. I was aware of her friendships with people like Hannah Arendt, and that before her husband's death she had known such men as Berenson, Loeser, Morgan, Frick, and the rest. Everything

considered, however—and everything in Ethel's case amounted
to a very great deal—it was not necessary in her company to
become acquainted with painters or men of letters, because she
herself so admirably embodied what was most precious in the
works and pleasures of the men and women who sustained our
companionship. They were the rare, great spirits of Western culture, and she was very like many of them.

These, then, are the fragments of memory meant to be pieced
together to form an imaginary frieze representing a situation
which provides matter for meditation that I had never thought
about till now. The figures of the frieze, though each is highly
individual, are nonetheless united not only in the composition
they form but also in the fundamental characteristics shared in
one way or another by all of them. Art or literature is the bond
that joins each to the next, both in action and in appreciation.
If friendship formed the cement of my memoirs, then fellowship
forms the mortar of my frieze, because most of these people
knew or met one another or, if they didn't, shared, understood,
and admired a common ideal. It was a golden age of aspiration
and innovation. What has become of it?

The frieze pieced together from my fragments appears not
only imaginary but mortuary now. Almost all the figures are
dead, and the few still living, like the author, before long will
be. The bits and pieces of their lives and creations will become
mere building blocks of structures inconceivable today. The artists and writers of another millennium, isolated in the quest for
uniqueness or the hunger for sensation, will wonder what it was
that once prompted Braque to say, "Picasso used to be a great
artist and now he's only a genius." Yes, the edifice of my memoirs is the memorial to a vanished world. The fragments of
memory are like shards unearthed on the sites of forgotten set-
tlements, spread out upon trestle tables, and studied by pains-

taking archaeologists in the vain hope of understanding how glorious it must have been to live when a gift for admiration could be not only bestowed but deserved.

Now my Envoi is nearly at an end. Before writing finis, however, I want to say a few words about my oldest friend, Bernard Minoret. He appears as an auxiliary character in a number of my memoirs, whereas in reality I have known him so well and for so long that he and his family and friends could easily provide matter for an entire volume. I have not wanted or endeavored to write it because it would entail too much autobiography and lead directly into the quicksands of ungrateful disclosure. There are those, however, Bernard himself among them, who have felt that I portrayed him shabbily, especially in certain passages of *Some Remarkable Men*, and I want to make it a matter of record that this was never my intention. Bernard is one of the most refined, intelligent, entertaining, and generous men I have had the good fortune ever to know. He has, to be sure, shortcomings and foibles. Who hasn't? But I wish publicly to proclaim that I respect, admire, and love him. To this declaration, I trust, he will respond with the good humor and goodwill which are so uniquely his own.

For my personal pleasure and satisfaction, I have saved for the next-to-last paragraph a few words of gratitude and esteem for my editor, friend, and collaborator, Jonathan Galassi. I believe Jonathan's judgment as an editor to be next door to infallible; his tact is exquisite, his good cheer invulnerable. My acquaintance with him, his sensitive, subtle wife, Susan, and their two delightful daughters has brought into the evening of my life a gleam of warmth and understanding.

Writing my volumes of memoirs has for me been interesting even if it hasn't invested my life with much interest. And, after all, now that it's done, after the frustrating quest for words, after the mornings, evenings, afternoons of tedium, after the plaints of the beloved companion to whom this volume, like the last one, is dedicated, I must admit that there have been occasional sparkles of satisfaction brought from faraway, unknown corners of the world, lit by letters from people I'll never know and had never heard of, people who thought they had found in my writings something to like, maybe even to admire. Only yesterday, in fact, I had a letter from a lady in Texas who had just read *Picasso and Dora* and in conclusion wished to "Thank you again for enriching my life." What measure of enrichment truly existed I cannot tell. That, perhaps, is irrelevant. One assumes, nevertheless, that if the lady took the trouble to write she was sincere. Then I owe her, and any other reader, the thankful assurance that despite intimations to the contrary I have written all these pages in the hope that fragments of authentic interest may actually be found among them.

Index

Acheson, Dean, 146
Acton, Arthur, 156, 158
Acton, Harold, 5, 158, 184
Aga Khan, 146
Albrizzi, Alessandro, 39
Angelico, Fra, 155
Angel of the Citadel, The (Marini), 100–1
Animal Farm (Orwell), 115
Aragon, Louis, 182
Arendt, Hannah, 164, 187
Arletty, 183
Arp, Jean, 89
Art and Literature magazine, 137
Art of This Century (gallery), 92–94, 98
Ashbery, John, 137
Astor, Brooke, 8
Astor, Vincent, 99
Atchley, Dana W., 146, 147, 149, 165
Atchley, Mary, 146, 147, 149, 165, 166

Auden, W. H., 186
Augustine, St., 180
Axelos, Kostas, 184
Axelos, Rhea, 184

Bache, Jules, 8, 156
Bacon, Francis, 44, 61, 63–65, 69, 70, 75, 77, 120, 122, 136, 186, 187; Giacometti and, 56, 58–60, 64, 72–73; Grand Palais retrospective of, 66, 76; Isabel Rawsthorne painted by, 50, 52, 71, 80; Leiris and, 133
Balthus, 79, 116, 182, 183, 185, 186
Barnes Foundation, 29–30, 99
Bartolo, Taddeo di, 150, 170
Bassano, Jacobo, 160
Baziotes, William, 94
Beast in the Jungle, The (James), 126
Beaumont, Etienne de, 183, 185
Beckett, Samuel, 62, 88

Beethoven, Ludwig van, 62, 184

Bellini, Giovanni, 155, 166

Berenson, Bernard, 156–58, 187

Bergson, Henri, 166

Bernard, Claude, 138

Bernard, Jeffrey, 72

Bernheim Jeune (gallery), 89

Birch, Patti, 129

Blake, William, 150, 160, 161, 167, 171

Blanchot, Maurice, 122

Bonsignori, Francesco, 155, 172

Boswell, James, 178

Botticelli, Sandro, 155

Bowles, Paul, 116

"Boy Who Wrote NO, The" (Lord), 116

Brancusi, Constantin, 89, 91, 99

Braque, Georges, 91, 119, 188

Brausen, Erica, 44, 63

British Museum, 122, 160

Britten, Benjamin, 186

Brockhurst, Gerald, 161

Burlington Magazine, The, 90

Burne-Jones, Edward, 161, 172, 174

Busch Quartet, 184

Cambiaso, Luca, 160, 161

Cameron, Rory, 13

Capote, Truman, 116

Caprara, Cardinal, 13

Caravaggio, 160

Carlyle, Thomas, 53

Cézanne, Paul, 12, 20, 22, 28, 144, 158, 186; Barnes and, 29, 99; in McIlhenny's collection, 5, 9, 29, 37–38, 40, 186; preser-

vation of studio of, 151, 171, 184

Chardin, Jean-Baptiste-Siméon, 5, 186

Chassériau, Theodore, 29

Chatsworth, 160

Chatwin, Bruce, 24

Chirico, Giorgio de, 91, 119

Christie's, 30, 33

City Square, The (Giacometti), 116

Clark, Kenneth, 24, 34, 186

Cloisters, 165

Cocteau, Jean, 89, 184–85

Condemned Playground, The (Connolly), 116

Confessions of an Art Addict (Guggenheim), 108

Connolly, Cyril, 113–19, 121, 123–24, 128, 130, 135–37, 140

Constable, John, 160

Corot, Camille, 29, 160

Countess de Tournon (Ingres), 34, 40

Craxton, John, 119–20, 124, 139, 186

Crivelli, Vittorio, 150

Cubism, 60

Curtis, Daniel, 95

Dalí, Salvador, 6, 31, 34, 185

Dance at the Moulin-Rouge, The (Toulouse-Lautrec), 9, 40

David, Jacques-Louis, 5, 13, 29, 40

Davillerd, Christian, 184

Death of Sardanapalus, The (Delacroix), 40

Degas, Edgar, 5, 29, 40, 78, 144, 160

Delacroix, Eugène, 9, 29, 40

Delmer, Sefton, 45

Derain, André, 55, 70

De Wald, Ernest, 162–63, 169–70

Diaghilev, Serge, 185

Dickinson, Emily, 151

Douglas, Langton, 156

Dubuffet, Jean, 59

Duchamp, Marcel, 89

Dunn, Anne, 137

Dunsany, Lord, 24

Duras, Marguerite, 60, 61, 63, 126, 130, 132, 134, 136

Dürer, Albrecht, 8

Duveen, Lord, 8, 145, 155

Duveen Brothers, 32

Dyer, George, 76

Eliot, T. S., 140, 186

Eluard, Paul, 182

Epstein, Jacob, 45, 70

Erasmus, Desiderius, 150

Ernst, Max, 91–93

Errazuriz, Madame, 185

Falkenstein, Claire, 109

Farouk, King, 123

Farson, Dan, 63, 64

Fischer-Dieskau, Dietrich, 30

Fitzwilliam Museum, 81

Four Saints in Three Acts (Stein), 183

Fouts, Denham, 118, 121

Fowler, Norman, 122–25, 127–29

Franchetti, Baroness, 38

Freud, Lucian, 69, 119–20, 133, 136, 139, 186, 187

Freund, Maria, 183

Frick, Helen, 157

Frick, Henry Clay, 99, 144, 145, 156, 187

Frick Collection, 165, 166

Fuseli, Henry, 160

Fussey, Henry, 11–14

Galassi, Jonathan, 189

Galassi, Susan, 189

Galerie Claude Bernard, 183

Gallagher, Patrick, 22, 38

Garbo, Greta, 24, 146, 186

Gardner, Isabella Stewart, 155, 158

Gatz, James, 24

Gauguin, Paul, 29, 160, 184

Gaviota (yacht), 14

Genet, Jean, 186

Géricault, Théodore, 29, 185

Giacometti, Alberto, 43, 53, 76, 77, 139, 185–86; Bacon and, 56, 58–60, 64, 72–73; Balthus and, 185, 186; biography of, 44–46, 54, 55, 65, 77, 137, 180; chandelier created for Horizon offices by, 117, 124; in Connolly's collection, 116; Isabel Rawsthorne and, 43–46, 48–51, 56, 57, 62–63, 66–71; in Peggy Guggenheim's collection, 91, 99; Sonia Orwell and, 133; Tate retrospective of, 43, 58; Watson and, 117, 119, 126, 187

Giacometti, Annette, 43, 55, 60, 62, 66, 68, 69, 71, 72, 76

Giacometti, Diego, 48, 50, 55, 56, 70–72, 76
Giorgio, Francesco di, 156
Gleizes, Albert, 99
Glenveagh Castle, 3–6, 14, 15, 19, 22–25, 30, 34–38
Golden Horizon, The (anthology), 117
Goodman, Paul, 116
Goya, Francisco, 60, 144, 183
Goyen, Bill, 113
Gozzoli, Benozzo, 164
Grandes Baigneuses (Renoir), 12
Grand Palais, 66, 76
Gravers, Robert, 180
Great Depression, 8, 32
Greco, El, 8, 185
Green, Julien, 185
Gris, Juan, 119
Guardi, Francesco, 160
Guercino, Il, 160, 161
Guernica (Picasso), 59
Guggenheim, Benjamin, 104
Guggenheim, Harry, 105
Guggenheim, Peggy, 85–110, 187
Guggenheim, Solomon, 89, 93, 104
Guggenheim Jeune (gallery), 89–90, 97
Guggenheim Museum, 93, 105
Guillaume, Paul, 183

Hamilton, Lady, 150, 161
Hansen, Waldemar, 121
Harvard University, 4, 5, 10, 159
Havemeyer, Mr. and Mrs. Horace, 156
Hayward, John, 186

Henderson, Wyn, 97
Heritage, Mrs., 12, 14
Hitler, Adolf, 90, 164
Hohnsbeen, John, 105, 109
Homer, 177
Horizon magazine, 114–20, 122–24, 135, 137

Ingres, Jean-Auguste-Dominique, 5, 22, 29, 34, 40, 144
Institute for Contemporary Art (ICA), 124, 127
Interior (Degas), 40

Jackson, Janetta, 127
James, Henry, 35, 38, 95, 126, 136, 157, 177, 179
John, Augustus, 160
Joyce, James, 177
Judgment of Paris, The (Renoir), 13
Julius II, Pope, 99

Kandinsky, Vassily, 89
Kant, Immanuel, 163
Kenmare, Lady, 13
Klee, Paul, 91, 99
Knoedler's, 32
Krasner, Lee, 94
Kress, Samuel, 156, 160, 171
Kuh, Fred, 86, 96
Kuh, Katherine, 86

Lacan, Jacques, 134
Lambert, Constant, 46, 80
Last Puritan, The (Santayana), 150
Lauder, Lady, 6
Laurencin, Marie, 184
Lawrence, T. E., 180

Léger, Fernand, 91
Lehman, Mr. and Mrs. Philip, 156
Lehman, Robert, 160
Leiris, Michel, 71, 133, 134
Leonardo da Vinci, 32, 122, 148,
    149, 160
Lindbergh, Charles, 146
Lizard, The (Lord), 101
Loeser, Charles, 156, 187
Longhi, Pietro, 39
López, Arturo, 14
Lorenzetti, Ambrogio, 156
Lorenzo the Magnificent, 99
Louvre, 160
Lucioni, Luigi, 161
Luini, Bernardino, 148, 151, 172
Lynes, George Platt, 32

Maar, Dora, 51, 101–2, 127, 182
McIlhenny, Frances, 4, 5, 9–10,
    32, 40
McIlhenny, Henry, 3–40, 186
McIlhenny, John, 7
Madame Cézanne (Cézanne), 39,
    40
Madeira, Louis, 12
Maeght, Marguerite, 70, 72
Magritte, René, 91
Maids of Honor, The (Velázquez),
    60
Manet, Édouard, 12, 29
Mann, Thomas, 85, 179, 181
Mantegna, Andrea, 155
Marcoussis, Louis, 99
Marcus Aurelius, 180
Margaret, Princess, 8, 186
Marini, Marino, 100–1
Martini, Simone, 156
Masaccio, 164

Massine, Leonid, 185
Masson, André, 134
Matisse, Henri, 5, 7, 29, 59, 186
Maugham, W. Somerset, 14, 184
Mellon, Andrew, 8, 155
Melville, Robert, 122
Menuhin, Yehudi, 15, 24, 30, 186
Menzies, Angus, 6, 13, 15
Merleau-Ponty, Maurice, 135
Messmore, Carmine, 32
Metropolitan Museum of Art
    (N.Y.), 165
Metropolitan Opera (N.Y.), 14
Michel, Albin, 107
Michelangelo, 99
Milton, John, 177
Minoret, Bernard, 97, 101, 124,
    125, 132, 189
Miró, Joan, 91
Models, The (Seurat), 29–32
Modigliani, Amedeo, 161
Mondrian, Piet, 59, 91
Monet, Claude, 29
Moore, Henry, 119
Morgan, J. P., 8, 145, 155, 156,
    187
Morrow, Mrs. Dwight, 145
Motherwell, Robert, 94
Moynihan, Rodrigo, 137
Museum of Modern Art (N.Y.),
    165
Mussolini, Benito, 103

Napoleon, 13
National Gallery (Washington,
    D.C.), 160
Nazism, 91
New York School, 94
New York Times, The, 108

Nicholas, Warwick, 55, 72
Night Thoughts (Young), 171
Nineteen Eighty-four (Orwell), 115
Noailles, Charles de, 12, 117
Noailles, Marie-Laure de, 11, 117, 183

Orcagna, Andrea, 158
Orwell, George, 113, 115, 123, 135, 138
Orwell, Sonia, 60, 61, 63, 113–40, 186–87
Out of This Century (Guggenheim), 86, 87, 108

Palazzo Venier dei Leoni, 100–5
Paolo, Giovanni di, 155, 162, 169–72
Parade, The (Seurat), 31–32
Parmigianino, Il, 160
Pears, Peter, 186
Perdikidi, Errieta, 184
Perkins, Mason, 156, 172
Pevsner, Antoine, 89
Philadelphia Museum of Art, 5, 10, 12, 40
Philadelphia Orchestra, 14
Picasso and Dora (Lord), 190
Picasso, Pablo, 7, 38, 52, 97, 125, 178, 188; Bacon on, 59; Cocteau and, 185; Dora Maar and, 102; Isabel Rawsthorne and, 55, 70, 71; in McIlhenny's collection, 6, 29, 31; in Maugham's collection, 184; in Peggy Guggenheim's collection, 99; politics of, 126, 182
Picasso, Paloma, 38
Piero della Francesca, 8, 155, 157

Pinturicchio, 164
Pitt-Rivers, Michael, 131–34, 136, 137
Pius VII, Pope, 13
Platt, Dan, 145, 146, 148–50, 152, 154–65, 168–69, 171, 172, 174, 187
Platt, Ethel Bliss, 143–74, 187–88
Points magazine, 101
Pollock, Jackson, 87, 93, 103
Pomeroy, Ralph, 86, 96
Pontormo, Jacopo da, 159, 160
Porter, Kingsley, 4
Poulenc, Francis, 183
Poussin, Nicolas, 129
Princeton University, 154, 159, 161–62, 168–70
Proust, Marcel, 166, 177

Raft of the Medusa (Géricault), 185
Rain (van Gogh), 10, 29
Raphael, 99, 155, 160
Rawsthorne, Alan, 46, 48, 50–57, 67, 187
Rawsthorne, Isabel, 43–81, 133, 187
Ray, Man, 183
Read, Herbert, 90
Realms of Being, The (Santayana), 150
Rembrandt, 8, 29, 61, 144
Renoir, Auguste, 5, 9, 12, 13, 29, 161, 184
Ricci, Sebastiano, 160
Richardson, John, 38
Richardson, Tony, 24
Rimbaud, Arthur, 62

Rodin, Auguste, 119, 160
Romney, George, 150, 161, 172
Roosevelt, Eleanor, 160
Roper, Lanning, 23
Rosa, Salvator, 150, 160, 161, 172
Rothko, Mark, 94
Roualt, Georges, 6
Rousseau, Henri, 29
Rousseau, Jean-Jacques, 180
Roy, Gilles, 38
Royal Academy (London), 44
Ruskin, John, 161
Russell, John, 44, 133
Russell, Véra, 44, 133–36, 140

Sachs, Paul J., 8, 10, 29
Sade, Marquis de, 122
Saint-Laurent, Yves, 183
Santayana, George, 150
Sarraute, Nathalie, 183
Sassetta, Stefano di Giovanni, 155, 160
Satie, Erik, 183
Schopenhauer, Arthur, 163
Searle, Alan, 184
Session of the Royal Company of the Philippines, The (Goya), 60
Seurat, Georges, 5, 29–33, 37–38
Signorelli, Luca, 164
Silberman brothers, 159–60, 162, 171
Six-Day War, 27
Skelton, Barbara, 117, 123, 124
Socrate (Satie), 183
Some Remarkable Men (Lord), 189
Soutine, Chaim, 29
Spanish Civil War, 115

Spender, Natasha, 24, 130, 186
Spender, Stephen, 24, 113, 118, 130, 135, 186
Stalin, Joseph, 90, 164
Stein, Gertrude, 180, 182
Steinlen, Théophile-Alexandre, 160
Still, Clyfford, 94
Stravinsky, Igor, 28
Sunflowers (van Gogh), 12
Sylvester, David, 44, 63, 133

Tanguy, Yves, 89
Tannhauser, J. K., 32–33
Tanning, Dorothea, 93
Tate Gallery, 43, 58, 80
Teresa, St., 185
Thomson, Virgil, 182–83
Through Italy with Car and Camera (Platt), 157
Tiepolo, Giovanni Battista, 150, 160, 161, 172
Tiepolo, Giovanni Domenico, 160
Titanic (ship), 87, 88
Titian, 8, 155, 158
Toklas, Alice B., 180, 182
Tolstoy, Leo, 177
Toulouse-Lautrec, Henri de, 6, 9, 32, 40, 184

Uffizi Gallery, 160
Unquiet Grave, The (Connolly), 116

Vail, Laurence, 91, 92, 98
Vail, Sindbad, 98, 101
van Gogh, Vincent, 10, 12, 22, 29, 34, 161
Vecchietta, Lorenzo, 155

Velázquez, Diego, 60, 144
Venice Biennale, 95
Vermeer, Jan, 60, 99, 144
Volpi, Count, 103
Vuillard, Édouard, 6

Walking Dead, 22
Warhol, Andy, 20, 22
Watson, Peter, 113–40, 186–87
Weidenfeld and Nicolson, 124,
    127
Welty, Eudora, 116
Westminster, Duchess of, 38, 186
Weyhe, E., 161
Wharton, Edith, 157
Where the Pictures Were (Lord),
    180
Wilde, Oscar, 9, 131

Wildenstein, Daniel, 171
Wildenstein, Georges, 32, 160,
    171
Wilder, Thornton, 183
Williams, Tennessee, 8
Wilson, Angus, 113
Windham, Donald, 116
Windsor Castle, 160
Wings of the Dove, The (James),
    38, 95
Wintersteen, Bernice (Bonnie)
    McIlhenny, 7–8, 10, 34, 39
World War II, 5, 10, 26, 45,
    178
Wright, Frank Lloyd, 93

Yale University, 169
Young, Edward, 171

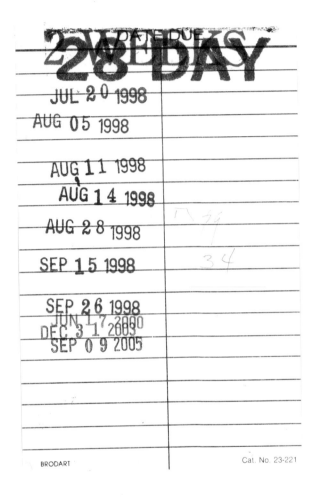